DAILY READINGS WITH MOTHER TERESA

My dear Kate

a very happy

With lo

Books in the same series

Daily Readings with William Barclay
Daily Readings with C. S. Lewis
Daily Readings with George MacLeod

DAILY READINGS WITH MOTHER TERESA

Edited by
TERESA DE BERTODANO

Fount
An Imprint of HarperCollins*Publishers*

Fount Paperbacks is an imprint of
HarperCollins*Religious*
Part of HarperCollins*Publishers*
77–85 Fulham Palace Road, London W6 8JB

First published in Great Britain
in 1993 by Fount Paperbacks
1 3 5 7 9 10 8 6 4 2

A catalogue record for this book is
available from the British Library

ISBN 0 00 627601 6

Set in Palatino by Avocet Typesetters, Bicester, Oxon

Printed and bound in Great Britain by
HarperCollinsManufacturing Glasgow

CONTENTS

Introduction	9
Make Me a Channel	19
Call Within a Call	20
Small Beginnings	21
The Home for the Dying	22
That I May Be Healed	23
All for God	25
First Steps	26
Going Home to God	28
Blessed Are the Lowly	29
Blessed Are the Poor in Spirit	31
Blessing and Persecution	32
Whatever You Did for the Least . . .	33
Love in Action	34
Surrender to God	35
Love Your Neighbour	36
Gifts of Love	38
Thirsting for Love	39
Sharing Christ's Passion	40
Another Nazareth?	42
One Heart Full of Love	43
I Am the Vine	44
The Chalice of Suffering	45
Blessed Are Those Who Mourn	46
Small Is Beautiful	48
Love of Poverty	49
Gift of God	51
Love Until It Hurts	53

To Love and to Share 54
Lighting the Lamp 55
Spiritual Poverty 57
Gifts of Love 58
Loving Compassion 60
Know the Poor 61
The Poverty of Loneliness 62
Take What You Need 64
Money Is Not Enough 65
The Greatest Scourge 66
In Tune with God 67
A Sign of His Love 69
Smile of Love 70
God Is the Source 72
Sanctity Is Simple 73
Conversion of Heart 74
Let God Use You 75
Thirsting for Peace 77
One with Christ 78
Rejoice in the Lord 80
The Least of My Brothers 81
The Bread of Life 82
The Joy of Loving 83
Who Is Jesus to Me? 85
Pray for the Patient 86
All Talk? 88
Love Begins at Home 89
Dream Big, Act Small 91
No Time? 92
Take Up Your Cross 93
Love to the Limit 95
My Brother, My Sister 97
The Beauty of Our Hearts 98
Be Still 99
Nicodemus 99

Touching the Body of Christ 100
Not for a Thousand Pounds 102
One Heart 103
Ask and You Shall Receive 104
Gift of God 106
Blessed Are the Peacemakers 107
In God's Care 108
Mother 110
The Purity of Mary 112
What Love Can Do 113
Friends of God 113
Paying the Price 114
Going Down the Ladder 115
Sunshine in Community 116
Hungry for Love? 117
I Love You 119
Learning to Pray 120
God's Grace, My Will 121
God Does Not Force Himself 122
The Prayer of Jesus 124
To Serve You 125
Fire of Love 126
Lord, Increase My Faith 127
Good and Bad 128
The Heart of the Home 129
Love Without Limits 131
The Vine and the Branches 133
Love for All Seasons 134
Keep Your Lamp Burning 135
Something Beautiful for God 137
Judge Not 138
Vision of Faith 139

INTRODUCTION

Agnes Bojaxhiu, known to the world as Mother Teresa of Calcutta, was born on 26th August 1910 in Skopje, Serbia. During her early years the only thing that distinguished Agnes was her "ordinariness" – even her youthful piety was nothing out of the way in a devout catholic family.

Agnes' parents, Dranafile and Nikola, were Albanians with a strong sense of national identity. Nikola was a successful businessman whose export interests took him around Europe, and on his return home Agnes and her older brother and sister would listen enthralled to the stories of his travels. Nikola also had strong political interests and was a firm supporter of the Albanian freedom fighters during the years leading up to the First World War, when relations between the two countries were deteriorating. In 1912 Albania's independence from Serbia was the occasion of great rejoicing in the Bojaxhiu household.

In 1919, when Agnes was eight, the happy family life came to an abrupt end with Nikola's sudden death. His business partner appropriated the assets of their joint concern, and the family were left with little more than the roof over their heads. Both parents had been anxious to ensure that their children sympathized with the plight of those poorer than themselves. Nikola's widow and her family were now to experience poverty at first hand. They not only survived but managed to remain happy and united.

As a child Agnes felt drawn to the poor, and at the age of twelve experienced a clear call to the religious life, although she was happy at home and her knowledge of convents was minimal. At that stage she had never even seen a nun – let alone spoken to one.

Africa had first captured Agnes' imagination but it was to India that her thoughts finally turned. Nuns of the international Loreto Congregation were working in Calcutta. Agnes applied for admission to the order, and in October 1928 left her homeland for a six-week stay in the Motherhouse of the Congregation at Rathfarnham, Dublin.

There is little in the years as postulant, novice and professed nun to excite comment. As a postulant in Ireland Agnes chose the name "Teresa" after Saint Thérèse of the Child Jesus, the nineteenth-century French Carmelite nun whose fidelity to God in the small things of daily life raised her to the heights of sanctity. Agnes was to be known as Sister Mary Teresa, and her six weeks in Ireland were spent steeping herself in the English language.

In December 1928 she left Dublin for Calcutta, arriving there on 6th January 1929. We are not told of her first response to the city which was to become her home and to which she drew the attention of the world. In fact she spent only one week there before going to join the other novices in the hills at Darjeeling, where she made temporary vows of poverty, chastity and obedience in 1931. After this she was sent to teach geography and history in one of the six schools run by the Loreto Sisters in Calcutta. During the early years in India she had to learn a third language – Bengali – in order to work in St Mary's High School for Bengali girls, in the same compound as the Loreto School. She became known as "the Bengali Teresa" to distinguish her from an Irish sister of the same name.

Two years after Teresa made her final vows as a Loreto Sister in 1937, the outbreak of the Second World War forced convents in Calcutta to evacuate their pupils. Those who could leave did so, although some of the children had no choice but to stay in the city. "The Bengali Teresa" remained with them to ensure that they did not miss out on an education. Sometimes they joined Teresa on her regular visits to the *bustees* or slum areas and a number of the girls were later to join Mother Teresa as the first members of her new Congregation, the Missionaries of Charity.

During the 1940s Teresa's health gave cause for concern. The Loreto Superior, fearing tuberculosis, ordered Teresa to rest in the hill station of Darjeeling. At some point on that journey Mother Teresa received the mysterious ''call within a call'', the anniversary of which is still celebrated by her sisters and Co-workers. When Teresa arrived in Darjeeling she knew she had to leave the security of her Convent and go out into the slums to live as one of the poorest of the poor and to serve those with whom Christ in St Matthew's Gospel had so specifically identified himself (Matthew 25: 35–36). In the 1940s, with her fragile health, she was an unlikely candidate for such a mission.

The only person to whom Teresa spoke of this ''call within a call'' was her Jesuit spiritual director, Father Celeste van Exem. He asked her to wait and in due course presented the request to the Archbishop of Calcutta who asked that she refrain from telling anyone, and himself expressed serious doubts about the advisability of any nun going out to live in the slums.

At this point the Archbishop fell seriously ill. Mother Teresa, who was impatient to begin her new life, sent a message saying that she would pray for him. If he recovered, would he take it as a sign that her call was from God and she was to start her new life? The Archbishop duly recovered but delays persisted. He finally permitted her to apply to the Mother General of Loreto for an Indult of Secularization which, if granted, would mean that on leaving the convent she would return to being a lay person.

Teresa's own wish was to leave the Convent while remaining a religious, but she obeyed the Archbishop. At

11

this point Mother Teresa would say that divine providence intervened. Both the Loreto Superior and later Rome ignored her request for an Indult of Secularization and gave her what she really wanted – an Indult of Exclaustration. This allowed her to leave the Convent while continuing to be bound by her vows.

On 16th August 1948, at the age of thirty-seven, Mother Teresa of Calcutta crossed the threshold of her Convent with a spare sari, five rupees and a train ticket to Patna. In Patna she would obtain a little medical training from the Medical Mission Sisters before starting work in the slums.

On her return to Calcutta she had to find a roof over her head. After much searching she obtained the free use of an upstairs room in a house owned by the four Muslim brothers called Gomez. From number 14 Creek Lane she set off each day to teach in her "school" – an open space among the shacks where she scratched letters of the alphabet in the mud for a growing number of pupils.

Spiritually and physically the early days were hard. Mother Teresa missed her old community life. She was lonely and frequently hungry. Little notes were left on the ground floor of number 14: "Mr Gomez, I have nothing to eat. Please give me something to eat." The Gomez family never failed her.

In March 1949 the first of Mother Teresa's former pupils knocked at the door of Creek Lane. The arrival of the future Sister Agnes heralded a steady flow of aspiring Sisters. By 1951 larger quarters were badly needed, and a Muslim leaving Calcutta for Pakistan found himself allowing the Sisters to have his house for less than the price of the land upon which it stood. Standing outside what is still the Motherhouse of the Congregation, he wept: "I received this house from God. I give it back to God."

Everything came in answer to prayer. There are stories of the Sisters having nothing for the evening meal until a

12

stranger arrived with several bags of rice. The needs of the poor were constantly met and it seemed that Mother Teresa had but to throw a medal of the Virgin Mary over the wall of a property on which her eye had lighted for it to become available for the work which she always insisted was not hers but that of God.

The Missionaries of Charity are known internationally for their work with the dying. Mother Teresa applied to the municipal authorities for a "house" for this purpose and was provided with pilgrims' dormitories attached to the Hindu Temple of the goddess Kali. This quickly became "Nirmal Hriday" or "Place of the Immaculate Heart", also known as "The Home for the Dying".

In 1955 Shishu Bhavan, the first children's home, was opened a stone's throw from the Motherhouse. Care for those suffering from leprosy was also a priority. They needed hospitals and mobile clinics but Mother Teresa was also concerned about the fear engendered by the disease. She began a campaign to raise awareness of the true facts under the slogan "Touch a leper with your compassion". Leprosy was not necessarily infectious. It could be treated and sufferers were able to return to the community if only their families would receive them back. She made it clear that it was not enough to give money – people needed to become personally involved with the poor.

The campaign succeeded beyond all expectation, and as well as raising awareness it generated enough money to open a major dispensary. The opening required a speech. The prospect filled Mother Teresa with dread, and she prevailed upon her friend and supporter Ann Blaikie to address the assembled well-wishers.

The partnership between these two women led to the establishment of the Co-Workers of Mother Teresa, a worldwide organization of lay people providing material and spiritual support for the Missionaries of Charity. The

Co-Workers have had a key role in the growth and effectiveness of the work, not least through the establishment of the "Sick and Suffering" branch. This network links a Missionary of Charity Sister or Brother with a "second self" who, although prevented by illness from taking an active part in the work, wishes to offer his or her sufferings to God for a particular Missionary of Charity and for the work undertaken by that Sister or Brother.

In Belgium, Mother Teresa's "second self", Jacqueline de Decker, co-ordinated the links between sick and suffering Co-Workers and the Sisters and Brothers. Mother Teresa herself depends greatly on the prayer and suffering of Jacqueline, and quotes the occasion when her "second self" was in great pain and facing the prospect of a very serious operation. Jacqueline believed this to be a sign that Mother Teresa had a particularly demanding year ahead of her, which proved to be the case.

At the end of the 1950s the work of the Congregation was still confined to the Archdiocese of Calcutta but the Missionaries of Charity were keen to spread their wings. Invitations were coming from other parts of India, including Delhi, and in 1959 the Archbishop of Calcutta allowed Mother Teresa to accept three of them. The Prime Minister, Jawaharlal Nehru, attended the opening of the children's home in Delhi. The support of Nehru and others ensured that news of the work spread more rapidly. Houses were even started in Bombay, where the residents had been reluctant to admit that their opulent city possessed slums.

In 1965 the new Congregation came under the direct authority of Rome, and in July of that year Mother Teresa and five Sisters set up the first overseas foundation in Venezuela. In 1968 Pope Paul invited them to work among the poor of Rome and more invitations poured in.

In the same year Mother Teresa was interviewed for

television by Malcolm Muggeridge during one of her first visits to London. Muggeridge knew nothing of this nun beyond the few facts he had been able to glean on the way to the studio, and technically the interview was a disaster. It went out on a Sunday evening, with phenomenal results. Money and letters poured in bearing the same message: "This woman spoke to me as no one ever has and I feel I must help her." The following year Muggeridge and a film crew left for Calcutta to make the film *Something Beautiful for God* which effectively ended any hope Mother Teresa might have had of personal anonymity.

In 1970, during a visit to London, she was taken to meet some of those sleeping rough under the railway arches and over the warm-air gratings. This experience coupled with increasing contact with the affluent countries of the West, led to her realization that the poorest of the poor were not necessarily those suffering the greatest physical deprivation. The poverty of the West was, if anything, a more difficult problem to solve. Christ was also crying out to be loved in the lonely, the drug addicts, the alcoholics and the neglected elderly people of Western countries.

The spiritual aspect of the work is paramount. In the poor for whom they care, Mother Teresa and her Brothers and Sisters believe that they are touching the broken body of Christ. Mother Teresa is the first to insist that the work is in no way related to the abilities of the Sisters. "Humanly speaking it is impossible, out of the question, because none of us has the experience. None of us has got the things that the world looks for. This is the miracle of all those little Sisters and people all around the world."

The avowed objective of every Missionary of Charity is "to satiate the thirst of Jesus Christ on the cross": that thirst which is the expression of Christ's need for love. It is this perception of the work which leads Mother Teresa to speak always of the privilege of caring for the poor, Christ's poor.

And she emphasises that "the poor" may include the materially comfortable who are also yearning for love.

The Eucharist is the principal means by which the Sisters and Brothers are sustained. Mother Teresa also stresses the indispensable need for prayer on which the action is totally dependent and the silence of the heart "in which God speaks". She insists that suffering in which she sees a special potency is essential to the whole. "Without our suffering, our task would be merely a social task, very beautiful and useful, but not Jesus's work. It would not be a part of the process of redemption."

It is perhaps surprising that Mother Teresa succeeds in "marrying" her conviction of the centrality of Christ and the rightness of Christianity with a deep respect for differing religious beliefs. She and the Sisters remain adamant that their purpose in all they do is to make a Hindu a better Hindu, a Christian a better Christian and a Muslim a better Muslim. In this, Mother Teresa is following the same precept as Charles de Foucauld, the French aristocrat who, in the early years of this century, abandoned a mis-spent army career to follow Christ in radical poverty among the Tuareg people of north Africa. A well-thumbed copy of *Seeds of the Desert*,[1] which is based on his teaching, is frequently beside her.

Although Mother Teresa describes herself as "the little pencil in God's hand", meaning that nobody looks at the pencil when reading a letter, she cannot escape the limelight, and her private wish to "retire" and work in the Home for the Dying is unlikely to be realized.

Despite attempts to stand down on grounds of age and ill health she was still Superior General of the Missionaries of Charity in 1992. Her travels were taking her ever farther afield, and the work had broadened to include people with AIDS in the USA and the destitute of Moscow and Georgia.

---

1. *Seeds of the Desert*, René Voillaume, Burns and Oates, London 1955.

By 1990 there were more than 3,000 professed Sisters in over 400 houses in just under 100 countries. The Missionary Brothers of Charity, founded in 1963, had approximately 400 professed members in 26 countries. In the 1970s a contemplative branch of the Sisters was established, and also a contemplative group of men. A branch was created for priests wishing to exercise their ministry in the spirit of Mother Teresa, and in 1989 the Lay Missionaries of Charity came into being for those who were married or single and wished to make an annual profession of private vows: poverty, (conjugal) chastity, obedience and wholehearted free service to the poorest of the poor. At the last count there were also three million Co-Workers in fifty-six countries.

The wheel came full circle in 1991 when "Nona Teresa" brought the Missionaries of Charity into Albania, to a jubilant welcome. She had longed to return years earlier when her dying mother had expressed the desire to see her youngest child. She had been unable to fulfil her mother's wish because there was no certainty that she would have been allowed to leave again. When she did return in 1991 Mother Teresa was touched to find that unknown hands had lovingly tended the graves of her mother and sister. She had come home, but only briefly, for now she belonged not to Albania but to the world.

*

Thanks are due to Mother Teresa for permission to use her material, much of which has previously appeared in Co-Worker Newsletters. Mother Teresa has never written a book so this selection is taken primarily from published transcripts of talks and public addresses, many of which are widely available. Where it has been possible to isolate a specific source this has been done. References to statistics in the text were accurate at the time the material was first made available but are not necessarily current.

A special debt of gratitude is due to Kathryn Spink without whose generous help and support this compilation could not have been made. Thanks also to the Benedictine communities of the Adorers of the Sacred Heart of Montmartre at Tyburn, London, and Wadhurst, Sussex, for their generous hospitality and the constant support of their prayers.

MAKE ME A CHANNEL

Daily Prayer of the Co-workers of Mother Teresa

Make us worthy, Lord, to serve our fellow men
    throughout the world
who live and die in poverty and hunger.
Give them, through our hands, this day their daily bread,
and by our understanding Love, give Peace and Joy.
Lord, make me a channel of Thy Peace,
that where there is hatred, I may bring Love;
that where there is wrong, I may bring the Spirit of
    Forgiveness;
that where there is discord, I may bring Harmony;
that where there is error, I may bring Truth;
that where there is doubt, I may bring Faith;
that where there is despair, I may bring Hope;
that where there are shadows, I may bring Light;
that where there is sadness, I may bring Joy.
Lord, grant that I may seek rather to comfort, than to be
    comforted,
to understand, than to be understood,
to love, than to be loved, for
it is by forgetting self that one finds,
it is by forgiving that one is forgiven,
it is by dying that one awakens to eternal life.

adapted from
The Prayer of Saint Francis

CALL WITHIN A CALL

In Skopje in Yugoslavia I lived at home with my parents; we children used to go to a non-Catholic school but we also had very good priests who were helping the boys and the girls to follow their vocation according to the call of God. It was then that I first knew I had a vocation to the poor.

At the beginning, between twelve and eighteen, I didn't want to become a nun. We were a very happy family. But when I was eighteen, I decided to leave my home and become a nun. I wanted to be a missionary, I wanted to go out and give the life of Christ to the people in the missionary countries. At that time some missionaries had gone to India from Yugoslavia. They told me the Loreto nuns were doing work in Calcutta and other places. I offered myself to go out to the Bengal Mission, and they sent me to India in 1929.

I took the first vows in Loreto in 1931. Then in 1937 I took final vows in Loreto. At Loreto I was in charge of a school in the Bengali department. At that time many of the girls that are now with me were girls in school. I was teaching them.

In 1946 I was going to Darjeeling, to make my retreat. It was in that train, I heard the call to give up all and follow Jesus into the slums to serve Him among the poorest of the poor. I knew it was His will, and that I had to follow Him. There was no doubt that it was going to be His work. But I waited for the decision of the Church.

I had first to apply to the Archbishop of Calcutta. Then with his approval the Mother General of the Loreto nuns gave me permission to write to Rome. I had to do this because I was a nun who had taken final vows and nuns cannot be allowed to leave the convent. I wrote to the Holy

Father, Pope Pius XII, and by return post I got the answer on the 12th of April. He said that I could go out and be an unenclosed nun under obedience to the Archbishop of Calcutta.

Something Beautiful for God
pp. 83–6

SMALL BEGINNINGS

In 1948 I left the Loreto convent and I went first to the Sisters in Patna to get a little training in medical work so that I could enter the houses of the poor; up till then I was only a teacher and I could not start on work with teaching. First I had to go into the homes and see the children and the sick. At the first little school I started on the first day there were five children. Slowly after that we had more and more children.

I began with teaching them their alphabet because, though they were all big children, they had never been to school and no school wanted them. Then we had practical lessons on hygiene; I told them how to wash themselves. Next day two or three girls came from the school where I had taught, they helped me with the children. Gradually the work started to grow and some ladies from Calcutta who had been teachers in the school where I had been teaching also came. And so the work started growing.

At first I had only five rupees, but gradually, as people came to know what I was doing, they brought things and money. It was all divine providence because right from the very first I didn't ask for money. It was all a gift. I wanted to serve the poor purely for the love of God. I wanted to give the poor what the rich get with money.

The Sisters started coming in 1949; the first Sister who joined our congregation was Sister Agnes. She is my assistant now. And the first ten girls who came were all students that I had taught in the school. One by one, they surrendered themselves to God to serve the poorest of the poor. They wanted to give their all to God.

Something Beautiful for God
pp. 87–90

THE HOME FOR THE DYING

In 1952 we opened the first Home for the Dying. One day when I went out I found a woman in a dustbin, and she was half eaten and I took her to a hospital, and they didn't want to take her, and I told them that I would stay at the hospital until they took her, and so to get rid of me I think, they took the woman. And the same day I went to the municipality and I asked for a house. I said I only wanted some place where I could bring these people, and the rest I will do myself. The official of the Calcutta Corporation took me to this place, a part of the Kali Temple, and he said, "This is the only place I can give you," and I said that this is just the ideal place because in this area there is not a Christian only Hindus and this is a very famous Hindu temple and people used to come there and worship and rest so I thought that this would be the best place for our people to be able to rest before they went to heaven; so I accepted there and then and within 24 hours the whole thing was arranged.

Those that have died there have died very beautifully – they have all died with God and content . . . because as one of them said, . . . "Thank God, I will die as a human being."

Then we have also the same kind of work for crippled and unwanted children. And there we get children picked up from the dustbins and drains and railways and so on . . . they are either brought in by people or by the Sisters themselves who pick them up . . . or by the police. At present we have never had so many. When these children come of school age we get sponsors for them to sponsor them for education and put them in the normal schools so that the children then feel normal like any other child. In England this was actually started by a Hindu lady who sponsored 10 children for 10 years and since then it has gone on.

Co-Workers' Newsletter

THAT I MAY BE HEALED

Since the nineteen-fifties we have been trying to work with the lepers and we have Hindu doctors who are voluntary workers with us and then we have our Sisters trained especially at the medical college for the work. And they go to those different centres and every week we get more and more new cases.

I really rejoice when they come because it is a good sign that they are beginning to feel that they want to be normal – they want to be like one of us – and very often we see a leper woman who is scarcely able even to walk, walking for miles, just to come to Sister to make sure that her child is all right. She has spotted the sign of leprosy in the child so she comes walking . . . all the way walking. We had the wonderful case of a woman who scarcely had any feet to walk on and she had walked more than six miles. And she came with this baby in her arms and said, ''Sister, see, my child has also got leprosy.'' She had seen a spot. The Sister examined the child and took the smear and all that but it was not leprosy and the woman, she felt so happy that her child didn't have leprosy she took the child and she walked all the way back – she didn't even stop to rest or anything, she was so happy that the child didn't have leprosy. That's a very beautiful thing that now they don't want their children to be disfigured so now they are coming in hundreds like that just to be able to help prevent the disease from growing.

If they come in time – what we call young cases – as soon as they discover that they have a spot or something they can be completely cured in a year or two and nobody will know that they have had the disease. Because in India the idea is, once a leper, a leper for life. And very often it happens there are broken homes, broken lives. Among our disfigured beggars are people who have been somebody in life. Last Christmas we had a Christmas party for all our lepers. Every leper got a parcel of food and clothes, and things like that. And at every centre we have made them choose their own leader, and they have their own council, so that we can deal with them when we have so many thousands in a group. So each leader is responsible for their own group. And this gentleman got up to thank the Sisters for what they had done for him and then he said, ''Some years back I was a very big man and I was working in offices in a large building; and I had air conditioning and people to answer my every call. I had people bowing to me when I used to come out of my office and I had a big family. But at once when they discovered that I was a leper all that has gone. There is no more air-conditioning, no fans, no home, no family, and only these young Sisters who wanted me and who are my people now."

And that is the story of most of our beggars.

Co-Workers' Newsletter

ALL FOR GOD

God has been very wonderful to us because as the work kept growing, our vocations also kept growing. In 1950, in October, the Holy Father made our little community into a Diocesan Congregation. Fifteen years later he raised it to a Pontifical Congregation; that means that we are now directly under the Holy Father. This has been the biggest miracle of all because as a rule congregations are not raised to the pontifical order so fast. It takes most of them many years, thirty, forty years sometimes, before they become a pontifical. This shows the great love and appreciation the Holy Father has for our work and for the congregation.

When the congregation became a diocesan congregation we were only twelve; that was in 1950. Gradually the numbers kept on increasing. For ten years we did not move out of Calcutta, because we had to train our Sisters for the work. In 1959, when we opened the first house in Dranchi and then one in Delhi, the numbers of Sisters started increasing and we began getting girls from the very places where we had opened houses.

These girls wanted to give their best, because in our Society we have to make a total surrender to God; this is the spirit of the community. They wanted to achieve this fulfilment in their own lives by giving all to God, giving up their position, their home, their future and dedicating all of it wholly to the poorest of the poor. They thought they couldn't give enough to God who had given them this beautiful vocation of serving the poorest of the poor.

From the day they join the community we spend a very good deal of time in training the Sisters, especially in the spirit and the life of the society which is beautifully defined in the constitution. This is the written will of God for us. Also, side by side with the spiritual training, they have to go to the slums. Slum work and this meeting with the people is a part of the noviciate training. This is something special to us as a congregation in order to be able to understand the meaning of our fourth vow, which promises that we give our wholehearted free service to the poorest of the poor – to Christ in His distressing disguise. Because of this it is necessary that the novices come face to face with the reality, so as to be able to understand what their life is going to be, when they will have taken their vows and when they will have to meet Christ twenty-four hours a day in the poorest of the poor in the slums.

Something Beautiful for God
pp. 93–7

FIRST STEPS

When girls come to us they join the aspirants. They spend about six months in seeing our work. They have to see if this is what God wants for them. And we have to see if they really have a vocation for this kind of life and work. At the same time they have to learn English because that is the language of our community, and as we do not have enough spiritual books in Indian languages we have to use English books. Also, in India we have so many languages, and the Sisters come from all over India, so it would be very difficult to train them in the spiritual life if there were so many languages being used in one community; so because of all this we have accepted to use English. After that they have to spend six months in postulancy where they begin to learn the rudiments of spiritual life. After these six months they join the noviciate for two years. During that time they have an intensive spiritual training in theology, Church history and the Scriptures, and especially in the rules and the constitution of our community. Because the Sisters are going to bind themselves by vows, they must know exactly what these vows are going to mean to them. The vow of poverty is very, very strict in our congregation because to be able to love the poor and to know the poor we must be poor ourselves. We take the vow of chastity, of giving our hearts complete and undivided to Christ – an entire dedication to Christ. We have also the vow of obedience and we take all the other vows according to obedience. We have to do God's will in everything. We also take a special vow which other congregations don't take, that of giving wholehearted free service to the poor. This vow means that we cannot work for the rich; neither can we accept any money for the work we do. Ours has to be a free service, and to the poor.

Something Beautiful for God
pp. 104–5

GOING HOME TO GOD

We help the poor die with God. We help them to say sorry to God. It is between them and God alone. Nobody else. Nobody has the right to come in at that time. We just help them to make their peace with God because that is the greatest need – to die in peace with God. We live that they may die, so that they may go home according to what is written in the book, be it written according to Hindu, or Muslim, or Buddhist, or Catholic, or Protestant, or any other belief.

Nobody in Nirmal Hriday has died depressed, in despair, unwanted, unfed or unloved. That is why I think this is the treasure-house of Calcutta. We give them whatever they ask according to their faith. Some ask for Ganges water, some for Holy Water, for a word or for a prayer. We try and give them whatever they want. Some just ask for an apple, or bread, or a cigarette. Others just want somebody to sit with them.

In the beginning we weren't accepted at all, we had quite a lot of trouble. At one time some young people were going around threatening and destroying and our people were getting more and more frightened. One day I said, ''If this is the way you want it, kill me, I will go straight to heaven. But you must stop this nonsense. You cannot go on like this.'' After that, it finished. It was all right.

We had one of the priests from the temple who died here very beautifully. The others could not understand because he was so bitter when he came in, very bitter and he was so young, only twenty-four or twenty-five. He was the head priest, I think. No hospital would take him in. He was thrown out. This is why he was so bitter. He did not want to die when he came, but he changed. He became quiet and peaceful. He was with us only two weeks and people from the temple used to come and visit him every day. They could not believe the change in him. I suppose, surrounded by people who were suffering in the same way, he learned to accept. The people themselves are of tremendous help to each other. I often wonder what would happen to the world if innocent people did not suffer so much. They are the ones who are interceding the whole time. Their innocence is so pleasing to God. By accepting suffering, they intercede for us.

Mother Teresa: Her People and Her Work
pp. 140–2

BLESSED ARE THE LOWLY

We consider it an honour and privilege to serve Christ in the distressing disguise of the poorest of the poor with our humble work. We do it with deep gratitude and profound reverence in a spirit of fraternal sharing, convinced that in accepting our humble service they make our existence as Missionaries of Charity possible.

Christ calls us through His Church to labour for the salvation and sanctification of the poorest of the poor all over the world and thus to satiate the thirst of God, dying on the cross, which is the thirst for our love and the love of souls by:

loving Him wholeheartedly and freely in the poorest of the poor with whom He identified Himself, both in our communities and in the people we serve, and so make His presence in them known, loved and served by all;

making reparation for sins of hatred, coldness, lack of concern and love for Him in the world today, in one another and in the people we serve.

Service means an unceasing and wholehearted labour in making ourselves available to Jesus so that He may live, in and through us, His life of infinitely tender, compassionate and merciful love, for the spiritually and materially poorest of the poor."

From the Rule of the Missionaries of Charity

Following the lowliness of Christ, we shall remain right on the ground:

by living Christ's concern for the poorest and the lowliest;

by being of immediate but effective service to them in all their needs, material and spiritual, until they can find some others who can help them in a better and more lasting way.

To fulfil our mission of compassion and love to the poorest of the poor we go seeking out in towns and villages all over the world even amid squalid surroundings, the poorest, the abandoned, the sick, the infirm, the leprosy patients, the desperate, the lost, the outcasts, taking care of them, rendering help to them, visiting them assiduously, living Christ's love for them, and awakening their response to His great love.

From an early draft of the Rule
Blessed Are You, pp. 60, 62, 64, 65

BLESSED ARE THE POOR IN SPIRIT

Christ, who being rich became poor and emptied Himself to work out our redemption, calls us:

to share in His poverty so that we might become rich through His poverty;

to bear witness to the true face of Jesus – poor, humble, and friend of sinners, the weak and the despised – and to the Church of the poor whose mission is to preach the Gospel to the poor;

to listen to the cry of the poor, especially in our times, which urges us to make reparation for the selfishness and greed of man, craving for earthly riches and power to the point of injustice to others.

Our response to the call of Christ is our vow of poverty. This entails a life which is poor in reality and in spirit, sober and industrious, and a stranger to earthly riches. It also involves dependence and limitation in the use and disposition of goods.

By this vow we freely give to God our natural right and freedom to accept and to dispose freely of anything that has a monetary value. Therefore, we shall never keep, give away, lend or borrow things of monetary value without leave of the Superior.

With regard to God, our poverty is our humble recognition and acceptance of our sinfulness, helplessness and utter nothingness, and the acknowledgement of our neediness before Him, which expresses itself as hope in Him, as an openness to receive all things from Him as from our Father.

Our poverty should be true Gospel poverty: gentle, tender, glad and openhearted, always ready to give as an expression of love. Poverty is love before it is renunciation:

To love it is necessary to give. To give, it is necessary to be free from selfishness . . . We rejoice with our Blessed Lady who sang so truthfully, "He has filled the hungry with good things, the rich He has sent empty away."

From the Rule of the Missionaries of Charity
Blessed Are You, pp. 28–31

BLESSING AND PERSECUTION

"Blessed are those who suffer persecution": To resist persecution, we need the continual refilling of prayer and sacrifice of the Bread of Life, of the living water, of our Sisters in community, and of the poor. We need Our Lady, our mother, to be with us always, to protect us and keep us only for Jesus.

Prayer enlarges the heart until it is capable of containing God's gift of Himself. Ask and seek and your heart will grow big enough to receive Him and keep Him as your own.

From a talk in Calcutta 1967

The Cross will be for us as it was for Christ: proof of the greatest love. Jesus alone, God made man, could fully understand the meaning of sin and suffer from it.

The force with which Christ was drawn to His Cross, in expiation for the sin of mankind, must urge us as Spouses of Jesus Crucified to accept voluntary nailing with Christ on the Cross, in a spirit of love, obedience and reparation for our own sinfulness and that of the world, especially our poor.

to fill up in our flesh what is lacking of the suffering of Christ on behalf of His Body, the Church;

to express our union and sharing in the sufferings of our poor, for their salvation and sanctification;

to give witness of penance so that the people of God will have the courage to accept it also in their own lives.

From the Rule of the Missionaries of Charity
Blessed Are You, pp. 128–9

WHATEVER YOU DID
FOR THE LEAST . . .

To bring Christ to others depends on how we do what we do for the poor. We could do it one way, or we could do it in some other way. I will never forget the time when a certain man visited our home for the poor who are dying. He arrived just as the Sisters were bringing in some of the dying off the streets. They had picked a man out of the gutter, and he was covered with maggots. Without knowing she was being watched, a Sister came to care for the dying man. The visitor kept watching the Sister work. He saw how tenderly she cared for her patient. He noticed how tenderly she washed the man and smiled at him. She did not miss a detail in her attentive care for that dying man. I was also at the Home for the Dying that day.

The visitor, after carefully watching the Sister, turned to me and said, "I came here today, not believing in God, with my heart full of hate, but now I am leaving here believing in God. I have seen the love of God in action. Through the hands of that Sister – through her gestures, through her tenderness – which were so full of love for that wretched man, I have seen God's love descend upon him. Now I believe." I didn't even know who this visitor was at the time, or that he was an atheist . . .

33

Do you want to do the same thing for those around you? You need to be united to Christ. You need prayer. Your service must come from a heart filled with God.

From a talk in London
June 1977
Blessed Are You, pp. 71–2

LOVE IN ACTION

"Whatever you do to the least of My brethren, you do to Me" (Matthew 25:40). If in My name, you give a glass of water, you give it to Me. If in My name, you receive a child, you receive Me (Mark 9:37).

He has made that as a condition also, that at the hour of death we are going to be judged on what we have been and what we have done. He makes Himself the hungry one, the naked one, the homeless one, the sick one, the lonely one, the unwanted one, the rejected one.

He says: "I was hungry and you gave Me to eat." Not only for bread, I was hungry for love. I was naked, not only for a piece of cloth, but I was naked for that human dignity of a child of God. I was homeless, not only for a home made of bricks, but I was homeless, rejected, unwanted, unloved, a throwaway of society, and you did it to Me." Jesus in the Eucharist made Himself Bread of Life to satisfy our hunger for God, for we have all been created to love and to be loved.

It is very clear what Jesus meant, because how do we love God? If we have been created to love, we all want to love God, but how? Where is God? God is everywhere. How do we love God? He gives us the opportunity to do to others what we would like to do to Him, to put our love for Him in a living action: loving and serving Him in the distressing

34

disguise of the poorest of the poor, both materially and spiritually, recognizing in them and restoring to them the image and likeness of God.

To a group of priests and from the Rule of the Missionaries of Charity
Blessed Are You, pp. 85–7

SURRENDER TO GOD

The religious life is going through a period of convulsion today. Believe me, my Brothers and Sisters in the religious life, everything will turn out all right if we surrender ourselves to God and submit ourselves to Him through obedience. Let us obey the Church. Let us obey the Holy Father who has a special love for us and truly desires us to be the bride of the crucified Christ.

We see ourselves surrounded by a thousand temptations that go against our vocation and against ourselves. There are so many changes and fads. That is not what is expected of us. Our young people have a burning desire to give themselves completely to God. For that very reason, they are afraid to embrace our way of life. They are afraid that while they are searching for this complete surrender to God, they will discover that this is not what we are offering them. Such problems don't exist only in Holland. They exist everywhere. That's why all of us should fall on our knees in the presence of the Blessed Sacrament and pray fervently.

Permit me to give you some advice: begin with the adoration of the Blessed Sacrament as the heart of prayer in your communities. Begin having it weekly, and you will see that soon the young Brothers and Sisters will ask if you can have it daily. Because as we advance in years, we experience a greater hunger for Jesus. The younger ones will encourage us through their magnificent example of sincere love for Jesus.

I receive many applications from many congregations. Many religious from different congregations want to join the Missionaries of Charity. I always tell them, "Truly live according to your rule. You will have no reason to change." Indeed, the constitutions approved by the Church have the written Word of God. Therefore, let us ask for the grace to remain faithful to our constitutions and to belong only to Jesus.

Pray for us that we won't spoil the work God has given us to do. As for me, I will pray and ask my Sisters to pray for you. We will pray that you may grow in holiness through faithfulness to your rules and constitutions that have been approved by the Church for the glory of God. There is no surer way to great holiness. May God bless you!

One Heart Full of Love
pp. 138–40

LOVE YOUR NEIGHBOUR

The streets of Calcutta lead to every man's door, and the very pain, the very ruin of our Calcutta, is heart's witness to the glory that once was and used to be.

I know you think you should make a trip to Calcutta, but I strongly advise you to save your airfare and spend it on the poor in your own country. It is easy to love people far away. It is not always easy to love those who live right next to us.

There are thousands of people dying for a piece of bread.

There are thousands upon thousands who die for a little bit of love, for a little bit of acknowledgement: Jesus is present in those who are hungry and falling under the weight of the cross.

People throughout the world may look different or have a different religion, education or position, but they are all the same. They are all people to be loved. They are all hungry for love. The people you see in the streets of Calcutta are hungry in body, but the people in London or New York also have a hunger which must be satisfied. Every person needs to be loved.

I see great poverty in the fact that in the West a child may have to die because we fear to feed one more mouth, we fear to educate one more child. The fear of having to feed an elderly person in the family means that this person is sent away. One day, however, we will have to meet the Lord of the universe. What will we tell Him about that child, about that old father or mother? They are His creatures, children of God. What will be our answer?

Have you ever gone to help the Missionaries of Charity or other Sisters in your own country? Or better still any charitable organization in the feeding programmes they have arranged for the destitute or hungry? If you have never gone, I think you cannot miss such as opportunity in life. It gives you the experience of sheer joy and fulfilment. You will get in touch with Christ, as you would do nowhere else.

We think we do so much for the poor, but it is they who make us rich. We are in debt to them.

Co-Workers' Newsletter
1988

GIFTS OF LOVE

The other day I went to Hyderabad to open a new centre. A Hindu gentleman, whom I had never seen before, was waiting for us with a surprise. He had decided to donate his house as a free gift to the Sisters. It was a beautiful house with a garden and everything else one could need. He had put it in our name without any strings attached. That is something beautiful that is beginning to happen more and more frequently.

Imperial Chemical Industries gave us a factory that used to manufacture all kinds of chemical products. I told them that this factory is now going to produce love, chemicals of love to help all sorts of people. And it really is producing love because so many people are becoming committed to serving the poor.

There are young people who come from all over the world to spend two weeks or a month working at the humblest of jobs out of love for others. They pick up all sorts of people off the streets for us, but they do it with a great deal of love. I feel unable to explain adequately what happens to those who lovingly serve the poor and what also happens to the people who are lovingly served. These homes of ours have become homes in which treasures of the kingdom are hidden.

In the same way, I hope that all the homes that we have opened will be our gift to you. They are gifts of love for your people. Through them, we hope to welcome many men and women in different areas who have nowhere to go because no one wants them. They have no one, and we want to offer them a home, a gift of love. We want to offer them a home where they can come and feel comfortable. We want to offer them a place where they can be loved and cared for, where their needs will be met.

One Heart Full of Love
pp. 97–8

THIRSTING FOR LOVE

Hunger is not only for bread. Hunger is for love. There are many many people, old people, crippled people, mentally ill people, people who have no one, nobody to love them. They are hungry for love. And maybe that kind of hunger is in your own home, in your own family. Maybe there is an old person in your family. Have you ever thought that you can show your love for God, by giving a smile, maybe just giving a glass of water, maybe just sitting there and talking for a little while?

There are many many like them in rich countries like Japan. The Sisters have found quite a lot of people who have forgotten what human love is because they have no one to love them. And so, begin to give the joy of loving, first in your family and to your next door neighbour. Maybe in your classroom, the girl that is sitting beside you, maybe she is feeling very lonely. Do you give her a smile? Maybe there is a child there beside you who cannot study as well as you. Do you help? This is the hunger, and sharing is a beautiful way of showing your love; showing that you really love God and your neighbour.

Jesus said: "I was naked and you clothed me." There are many people in very cold countries, poor people who have nothing, who have died, frozen because they have no clothes. But there is a much greater nakedness: the loss of human dignity, the loss of that beautiful virtue, purity. This is a great nakedness and there you can share with them. Pray for them, make sacrifices and protect your own purity so that you'll always remain covered with the joy of purity.

And then we have homelessness. I don't see in the streets of Tokyo people lying in the street. I have not yet seen anybody like that. But homelessness is not only want of a house made of bricks. There are many people, the

39

drunkards, the drug-addicts, people who feel unwanted, unloved in a throwaway society. Oh! that one is a mental case. Out! That one is very stupid. Out! This is homelessness and this is where we have to see, to look and do something. You see a blind person, crossing the road. That is homelessness. You come, take the hand, walk with that person. Or a mental case. We are inclined to laugh at the mental cases. But don't laugh. Go, hold, help, be kind, be compassionate. Jesus will say to you: I was homeless and you took me in. You befriended me, you loved me, you took care of me . . . This is love in action.

Co-Workers' Newsletter
(from a speech to Japanese schoolchildren) 1985

SHARING CHRIST'S PASSION

There is hunger for ordinary bread, and there is hunger for love, for kindness, for thoughtfulness; and this is the great poverty that makes people suffer so much.

Suffering in itself is nothing: but suffering shared with Christ's passion is a wonderful gift. Man's most beautiful gift is that he can share in the passion of Christ. Yes, a gift and a sign of His love; because this is how the Father proved that He loved the world – by giving His Son to die for us.

And so in Christ it was proved that the greatest gift is love: without Him we could do nothing. And it is at the altar that we meet our suffering poor. And in Him that we see that suffering can become a means to greater love, and greater generosity.

Without our suffering, our work would just be social work, very good and helpful, but it would not be the work of Jesus Christ, not part of the Redemption. Jesus wanted to help by sharing our life, our loneliness, our agony, our death. Only by being one with us has He redeemed us. We are asked to do the same; all the desolation of the poor people, not only their material poverty, but their spiritual destitution, must be redeemed. And we must share it, for only by being one with them can we redeem them by bringing God into their lives and bringing them to God. Suffering, if it is accepted together, borne together, is joy.

If sometimes our poor people have had to die of starvation, it is not that God didn't care for them, but that you and I did not give, were not an instrument of love in the hands of God, to give them bread, to give them clothing. We did not recognize Him, when once more Christ came in distressing disguise, in the hungry man, in the lonely man, in the homeless child seeking for shelter.

God has identified himself with the hungry, the sick, the naked, the homeless. Hunger is not only for bread, but for love, for care, to be somebody for someone. Nakedness is not only the need for clothing, but the need for the compassion which very few people give to the unknown; homelessness is not just the need for a shelter made of stone, but having no one to call your own.

Co-Workers' Newsletter
1981

41

ANOTHER NAZARETH?

I don't need money from your abundance. I want you to share the work. I want you to touch, to understand. Come, when we have the people here, come and see. This evening I met some of our people that come here for supper. They are such loveable people. They thank from the bottom of their hearts. They have nothing. We didn't give them anything much, just a few sandwiches and a cup of tea – not much. But what they felt – that they are wanted, that there's a place where they can come, that they can see that they are loved, that they are respected. And this is something that I want you to share. There must be that difference in a Co-Worker, that sharing. Small things. I don't want you to give from your abundance. I want you to give like the little child who said, "For three days I will not eat sugar – I will give my sugar to Mother Teresa" – such a small thing.

And this is what I want you to feel, to enjoy. You have to experience to be able to understand what I am saying. I've had to experience it to be able to understand it. The same thing for each one of you. You must experience it in your own home first. You must make your house, your family, another Nazareth, where love, peace, joy, unity reign. And then you will be able to reveal that and to give it to your next door neighbour.

That's why I beg of you: try to find your poor here, first in your own home. Don't allow anybody to be lonely, to feel unwanted, unloved, but especially your own, especially your neighbour. And then someone who is blind. Just go and read the newspaper, just do some shopping for somebody, just go and clean a little bit, nothing more.

From Mother Teresa's talk to the Co-Workers of
Liverpool at the opening of the Sisters' new Centre
May 1979

ONE HEART FULL OF LOVE

Gifts should be the spontaneous giving of those who are not afraid to love till it hurts. Giving need not be confined to money or material gifts, but I would like more people to give their hands to serve and their hearts to love – to recognize the poor in their own homes, towns and countries, and to reach out to them in love and compassion. The International Association of Co-Workers is an opportunity for lay people to grow in the likeness of Christ through humble works of love and service in their own families first; their next door neighbours in the city in which they live; and in the world. Thus they share in the spirit of our Society, and, with the Missionaries of Charity, they become carriers of God's love and compassion. I believe that God loves the world today through us and all who share in work with us.

Let us, all of us, just be of one heart full of love so we can really spread that sanctity, that holiness, because holiness is not the luxury of the few; it is meant for each one of us. I think only holiness will be able to overcome evil and overcome all the suffering and miseries of the people – and of our own life, also. We too have to suffer, and suffering is a gift of God if we use it in the right way. The cross must be there, and so let us thank God for this.

So let us all make that one resolution that we will be all love to Jesus in the world; that we will allow Him to love in us and through us and that we will be at His disposal to make use of us without consulting us. I think that is the best way to show our love for Him, to accept Him as He comes. If He wants to come into our life in humiliation, in suffering, all right. If He wants to come in publicity, all right. Whatever it be, success, failure, it makes no difference to Him, and it should not make a difference to us either. Health and sickness, they come from the same loving hand. To be able to accept whatever He gives and to be able to give whatever He takes with a big smile — that is holiness for you and for me.

Co-Workers' Newsletter
1982

I AM THE VINE

In every country the Co-Workers have a chairman, or president, but the name I want to use is something very simple. I would rather like to use a "link" — like a branch, a link, a joining. I would like the fifteenth chapter of St John to become like our life. Jesus has said, "I am the vine and you are the branches", so let us all be like the branch. The Society of the Missionaries of Charity is the branch and all the Co-Workers are the small branches joined to that one branch and we are all joined to Jesus. I think that is the best picture of what we are supposed to be in the world. All the different links in different countries are all joined to that one branch, the Society of the Missionaries of Charity, and the Missionaries of Charity are joined to the one Jesus. And all the fruit is in the branches in each of the countries. It is a very beautiful, living picture of what we, the Missionaries of Charity and Co-Workers should be, joined completely, and let us not forget that it is on the branch that the fruit is, not somewhere else. All of you must be joined, you must know each other and you must be linked like that, and I feel that will really bring tremendous presence to the world.

We depend on Divine Providence and I do not want people to get the idea that we are after their money, and that we want their money, that we are just a group of men and women and children to see how much we can get out of them. This is the last thing in my mind. I want it to be the last thing in your minds also. Let us not give the impression either that we work for how much we can gather, how much we can spend, how much we have in the bank. The Co-Workers also must depend on Divine Providence. If the people give it thank God, but please do not have regular things that will lead you to spend time in raising money, in making money. I would rather you spent the time in real service to the people. And no advertising, no writing letters to beg for money, no making things for selling. Let us bring a spirit of sacrifice into the lives of our people. I think Jesus wants us to be like this and I will repeat it again and again if necessary. Let us offer all this work now for the glory of God, and also that we may be able to become instruments of peace of love, of compassion.

From a meeting of Co-Workers
Germany August 1976

THE CHALICE OF SUFFERING

Amongst our Co-Workers we have sick and crippled people who very often cannot do anything to share in the work. So they adopt a Sister or a Brother, offering all their sufferings and all their prayers for that Brother or that Sister, who then involves the sick Co-Worker fully in whatever he or she does. The two become like one person, and they call each other their second self. I have a second self like this in Belgium, and when I was last there she said to me: ''I am sure you are going to have a heavy time, with all the walking and working and talking. I know this from the pain

I have in my spine, and the very painful operation which I shall shortly need to have." That is her seventeenth operation, and each time that I have something special to do, it is she behind me that gives me all the strength and courage to do what I have to do to fulfil God's will. This is why I am able to do what I am doing; as my second self, she does all the most difficult part of the work for me.

My very dear suffering Sisters and Brothers, be assured that every one of us claims your love before the throne of God, and there every day we offer you, or rather offer each other, to Christ for souls. We, the Missionaries of Charity, how grateful we must be − you to suffer and we to work. We complete in each other what is lacking in our relationship with Christ. Your life of sacrifice is the chalice, or rather our vows are the chalice, and your suffering and our work are the wine − the spotless heart. We stand together holding the same chalice, and so are able to satiate His burning thirst for souls.

A Gift for God
pp. 29−31

BLESSED ARE THOSE WHO MOURN

Suffering is nothing by itself, but suffering that is shared with the passion of Christ is a wonderful gift and a sign of love. God is very good to give you so much suffering and so much love. All this becomes for me a real joy, and it gives me great strength because of you.

It is your life of sacrifice that gives me so much strength. Your prayers and suffering are like the chalice in which those of us who work can pour the love of the souls we encounter. So you are just as necessary as we are. We and you together can do all things in Him who strengthens us. Your vocation as suffering Co-Workers is so beautiful: you are messengers of God's love. We carry in our hearts the love of God, who is thirsty for souls; you can quench His thirst through your incomparable suffering, to which our hard work is united. It is you who have tasted the chalice of His agony.

Without our suffering, our task would be merely a social task, very beautiful and useful, but not the work of Jesus. It would not be a part of redemption.

Jesus has wished to offer us His help by sharing our life, our loneliness, our agony, our death. It was necessary for Him to become one with us in order to save us.

We are allowed to do likewise. The afflictions of the poor, not only their material misery but also their spiritual lowliness are to be redeemed. We have to share these afflictions, since only by becoming poor will we be able to save them – that is, to bring God into their lives and to bring them to God.

When suffering comes close to us, let us accept it with a smile. This is God's greatest gift: having the courage to accept with a smile all he gives us and all he requires of us.

Sacrifice, in order to be genuine, has to empty us of ourselves.

We often say to Christ, make us partakers of your suffering. But, when someone is insensitive to us, how easily we forget that this is the moment to share with Christ! It would be enough for us to remember that it is Jesus who gives us, through such a person or circumstance, the opportunity to do something beautiful for Him.

From a meeting of Co-Workers
Germany, August 1976
Blessed Are You, pp. 43–6

SMALL IS BEAUTIFUL

I do not agree with the big way of doing things. To us what matters is an individual. To get to love the person we must come into close contact with him. If we wait till we get the numbers, then we will be lost in the numbers. And we will never be able to show that love and respect for the person. I believe in person to person; every person is Christ for me, and since there is only one Jesus, that person is the only person in the world for me at that moment.

I believe the people of today do not think that the poor are like them as human beings. They look down on them. But if they had that deep respect for the dignity of poor people, I am sure it would be − it would be easy for them to come closer to them, and to see that they, too, are the children of God, and that they have as much right to the things of life and of love and of service as anybody else. In these times of development everybody is in a hurry and everybody is in a rush, and on the way there are people falling down, who are not able to compete. These are the ones we want to love and serve and take care of.

We ourselves feel that what we are doing is just a drop in the ocean. But if that drop was not in the ocean I think the ocean would be less because of that missing drop. For example, if we didn't have our schools in the slums − they are nothing, they are just little primary schools where we teach the children to love the school and to be clean and so on − if we didn't have these little schools, those children, those thousands of children, would be left in the streets. So we have to choose either to take them and give them just a little, or leave them in the street. It is the same thing for our Home for the Dying and our home for the children. If we didn't have that home, those people we have picked

up, they would have died in the street. I think it was worth while having that home even for those few people to die beautifully, with God and in peace.

Something Beautiful for God
pp. 118–19

LOVE OF POVERTY

One loses touch with God when one takes hold of money. God preserve us. It is better to die. What would one do with surplus money? Bank it? We must never get into the habit of being preoccupied with the future. There is no reason to do so: God is there. Once the longing for money comes, the longing also comes for what money can give: superfluous things, nice rooms, luxuries at the table, more clothes, fans, and so on. Our needs will increase, for one thing leads to another, and the result will be endless dissatisfaction.

If you ever have to get things, you must buy things of cheaper quality. We must be proud of being poor. Pay attention to the little fox that sneaks in after us. We may carry water upstairs for a bath and find three buckets already full in the bathing room. Then the temptation comes to use all the water . . .

If you have to sleep in a corner where there is no breeze, do not gasp and pant to show how much you feel it. In these little things one can practise poverty. Poverty makes us free. That is why we can joke and smile and keep a happy heart for Jesus . . .

Some Sisters seem to be in a continual, feverish excitement about money for their work. Never give the impression to

people when you beg that you are out to gather money. Let your work speak. Let your love for the people enkindle the rich people's hearts. They will give if you don't grab. Even if you have to beg, show that your heart is detached by being at ease, both when they refuse you and when they give.

A rich man of Delhi said: "How wonderful it is to see Sisters so free from the world, in the twentieth century when one thinks everything is old-fashioned but the present day."

Keep to the simple ways of poverty, of repairing your own shoes, and so forth, in short, of loving poverty as you love your mother. Our Society will live as long as that real poverty exists. The institutes where poverty is faithfully practised are fervent and need not fear decay. We must always try to be poorer still and discover new ways to live our vows of poverty. We must think ourselves very fortunate if we get a few chances in life to practise this wonderful poverty. . . . To rejoice that others are more fortunate than we takes much virtue . . .

When St Francis of Assisi heard that a new rich house had been built for the brethren, he refused to enter the city . . . We must not spend time and energy on the house by making it look attractive and beautiful. God save us from such convents where the poor would be afraid to enter lest their misery be a cause of shame to them.

When we dress ourselves we should with devotion remember what each article of the religious habit means to us: the sari with its blue band is a sign of Mary's modesty; the girdle made of rope is the sign of Mary's angelic purity; sandals are a sign of our own free choice; and the crucifix is a sign of love.

. . . Sisters shall live by begging alms. We depend entirely on the charity of the people. The Sisters should not be ashamed to beg from door to door if necessary. Our Lord

Himself has promised a reward even for a cup of water given in His name. It is for His sake that we become beggars.

In fact He often endured real want, as the stories of the multiplication of the loaves and fishes and the plucking of the ears of corn on walks through the fields teach us. The thought of these instances should be salutary reminders whenever in the mission or at home our meals are meagre . . . Our Lord on the cross possessed nothing . . . He was on the cross that was given by Pilate. The nails and the crown were given by the soldiers. He was naked and when He died, cross, nails, and crown were taken away from Him. He was wrapped in a shroud given by a kind heart, and buried in a tomb that was not His. Yet Jesus could have died as a king and He could have risen from the dead as king. He chose poverty because He knew in His infinite knowledge and wisdom that it is the real means of possessing God, of conquering His heart, of bringing His love down to this earth.

The Love of Christ
pp. 106–8

GIFT OF GOD

Jesus said, "You are more important to my Father than the lilies of the field, the grass and the birds" and it has come true. There has not been one single day that we have refused *anybody*, that we did not have food, that we did not have a bed or something, and we deal with thousands of people. We have 53,000 lepers and yet never has one been sent away because we did not *have*. It is always there, though we have no salaries, no income, no nothing, we receive freely and give freely. This has been such a beautiful gift of God. In so many ways we have seen the delicate thoughtfulness of God. In Calcutta alone we cope with 7,000 people every day and if one day we do not cook they do not eat. One Friday morning Sister came and told me: "Mother, Friday, Saturday there is no food. We will have to tell the people we have nothing to give today and tomorrow."

I had no words, I had nothing to say to her but by 9 o'clock the Government for some unknown reason, had closed all the schools and all the bread that would have been given to the children was sent to us and our children and our 7,000 people ate bread and bread for two days. They had never eaten so much bread in their lives! Nobody in the whole city knew why the schools were closed but I knew. I knew the delicate thoughtfulness of God, such a delicate love. So let us believe in His love, in His faithful love. When you look at the cross you will see His head bent down to kiss you. You will see His hands extended to embrace you. You will see His heart open to receive you. Be not afraid, He loves you and He wants us to love one another as He loves us. As miserable as we are, as sinful as we are, He loves us. His love is faithful and we must believe in His love. And if we really believe it we will find the poor right in our home. A few days ago our Sisters went out at night – they go out at night to work, to pick up the people on the streets. They saw a young man there, late at night – lying in the street and they said, "You should not be here, you should be with your parents," and he said, "When I go home my mother does not want me because I have long hair. Every time I went home she pushed me out." By the time they came back he had overdosed himself and they had to take him to hospital. I could not help thinking it was quite possible his mother was busy, with the hunger of our people of India, and there was her own child hungry for her, hungry for her love, hungry for her care and she refused it. Bring love into your home. If you really love God begin by loving your child, your husband, your wife.

From Mother Teresa's address in Dublin
June 1979

LOVE UNTIL IT HURTS

A gentleman came to our house and he told me, "There is a Hindu family with about eight children who have not eaten for a long time." So I took some rice quickly and went to their family and I could see real hunger on the small faces of these children and yet the mother had the courage to divide the rice into two and she went out.

When she came back, I asked her, "Where did you go? What did you do?"

And she said: "They are hungry also."

"Who are they?"

"The Muslim family next door with as many children."

She knew that they were hungry. What struck me most was that she knew and because she knew she gave until it hurt. This is something so beautiful. This is living love. She gave until it hurt. I did not bring more rice that night because I wanted them to enjoy the joy of giving, of sharing. You should have seen the faces of those little ones. They just understood what their mother did. Their faces were brightened up with smiles. When I came in they looked hungry, they looked so miserable. But the act of their mother taught them what true love was. This is the greatness of our poor.

One night in Calcutta we picked up some patients from the street and one of them was in a very terrible condition and I told the sisters: "I'll take care of her." And I took care of her and all that my love could have done, I did for her. When I put her in bed, she took hold of my hand. There was a very beautiful smile. I have never seen a smile like that on a human face. There was a beautiful smile on her face and she said two words only: "Thank you," and she died. For a second I reflected, looking at her and I said: "If I was she what would I have done?" And my sincere answer was, I would have tried to draw a little attention to myself. I would have said, "I'm cold" or, "I'm hungry" or, "I'm dying" or something. But this wonderful woman, she gave me more than I gave her. She gave me her understanding love. These are our people. Do you know them? They may be in your own home. The lonely people are everywhere. Do we know them?

From an address in Malta to the
World Congress of the Lasallian Foundation
August 1976

TO LOVE AND TO SHARE

A very poor woman came to me and said, "I would like to share with you, to help you in the work, I am a washerwoman and I go and wash clothes. Could I come once a week and wash clothes in the children's home?" Now that means money for her, that means sacrifice for her, and I said "by all means" . . . Then I had another experience. We travel by second-class tram and I was in the tram and this gentleman walked up to me and said, "Are you Mother Teresa?" and I said, "Yes". He said, "I have been longing to share in your work but I am very, very poor.

Will you allow me to pay your ticket for you?'' If I refused him, it would hurt him, and if I accept maybe he will give everything he has, but it is better to take what he has than to hurt him, so I said, "Yes". Then he took out a dirty piece of cloth and there inside was the fare. He gave it to the conductor and he paid the ticket for me. He was supremely happy and he said, "At last, I have been able to share.'' Well, then he may have had to go without food or maybe he would have had to walk a long distance, but there was the joy of this wonderful man who wanted to share and he did share in this work of love.

From an address to Co-Workers in the USA 1974

LIGHTING THE LAMP

In Australia we have a home for the alcoholics and the Sisters picked up a man from the street who had been an alcoholic for many years. He had ruined his own life and the lives of his children and family and everything. Then, suddenly one day he realized that God loved him. It was because of the way the Sisters talked to him, the way they touched him, the way they loved him. They didn't do anything special but the way they dealt with him, with so much love, so much compassion, so much understanding: not a bit surprised that he was a drunkard, that he was so helpless, that he was so hopeless. Then suddenly this "God loves me", and from that day he never touched drink again. He went back home, went back to his family and back to his job and everything. Then when he got the first salary he took the money and he went to the place where we are building a rehabilitation centre for the homeless alcoholics, especially for the old people who are kept in prison just because if they let them out they have no place to go so they drink. We want to take these people from the jail and give them a home and make them feel loved and cared for. He went and brought his salary there and said, "God has been so wonderful to me. In the Sisters and through the Sisters I have come to know that God loves me. This has brought me back to life and I want to share that life with others."

Also in Australia we found an old man in a most terrible condition and so I went in there and tried to talk to him and then I said to him: "Kindly allow me to clean your place and clean your bed and so on", and he said, "I'm all right", and I said to him: "You will be more all right if I clean your place". Anyway, at the end he allowed me to do it. When I was in his room – I call it a room but it was not really even a room – I saw that he had a lamp, a very beautiful lamp but covered with dirt and dust and I said to him, "Do you not light the lamp?" and he said, "For whom? Nobody comes, I never see anybody. Nobody comes to me. I don't need to light the lamp." And I asked him, "If the Sisters come to you, will you light the lamp for them?" And he said, "Yes." So the Sisters started going to him in the evening and he used to light the lamp, to clean the lamp. After more than two years, he sent me word through the Sisters and he said, "Tell my friend, the light she lit in my life is still burning." That was such a small thing but in that darkness of loneliness, a light was lit and that light kept on burning.

Give . . . Give to your neighbour the love that you have received. True love must hurt. That is why we must give until it hurts, with our time, with our hands, with our minds, whatever we have, in that sharing.

Co-Workers' Newsletter

SPIRITUAL POVERTY

Some time ago, a little child came to our house about midnight and I went down and this little one was crying and said: "I went to my mother, my mother didn't want me. I went to my father and my father didn't want me. You want me."

This is a picture that is being re-enacted every day in many places.

Here also in Melbourne, we have people who are not wanted, who are not loved, and they are His, they are He. And they are ours. They are our Brothers and Sisters.

In India, in Europe, in all the places, wherever the Sisters are meeting with Christ in the distressing disguise, it is the same hunger. Maybe here in Australia and in Europe and in America, we don't have hunger for a slice of bread, for a piece of cloth, but there is that terrible loneliness, there is that terrible sense of not being wanted, not being loved, having no one to call your own.

This is great poverty and we must believe Christ, who cannot deceive us and who said, "I was hungry and you gave me to eat. I was naked and you clothed me. I was homeless and you took me in . . . you did it to me."

In Calcutta, we have picked up over 27,000 people from the streets. They come to us, we pick them up, we bring them to our shelter. They die so beautifully, they die so beautifully with God. Up to now I have never yet seen or met, nor have the Sisters seen, any man or woman refuse to say "sorry" to God, refuse to say, "I love you, my God".

We have those thousands of lepers. They are so great, they are so beautiful in their disfigurement. Last Christmas, I went to them (we give them a Christmas party every year – there are thousands of them) and I told them that what they have is the gift of God, that God has a very special love for them, that they are very dear to Him, that what they have is not sin.

An old man who was completely disfigured, tried to come near me and he said, "Repeat that once more. It did me good. I've always heard that nobody loves us. It is wonderful to know that God loves us. Say that again."

Here in Melbourne we have a home of compassion. We have people who have no one, who roam the streets, for whom maybe only gaol and the road are the only places. And one of them was very badly hurt by another friend of his, another companion. Thinking that the matter was very serious, somebody asked him, "Who did that to you?" And the man started telling all kinds of lies, but he wouldn't give the name. And after the person had gone away, I asked him, "Why did you not tell who hurt you?" And the man looked at me and said, *"His suffering is not going to lessen my suffering."*

This is "Love one another as I have loved you."

From an address to the Conference on Population and Ecology
Melbourne, Australia, 1973

GIFTS OF LOVE

In Venezuela the Sisters are working in the interior. They had a charity week – one day for the children, and one day for the sick, and one day for the old. So the day we had for the sick we made little parcels for them – and I saw one woman whose knees were touching her face, she was just completely crippled and no one to look after her. We have our Co-Workers there also, so I said, "The only thing that you could give me is to get me a house for these people so that we can take care of them. And the Chairman of the Co-Workers, very well-to-do, went home and she was after her husband morning, noon and night, till at the end the poor man had to give in and he happened to have a house, an old house, in the place where we are staying. And without telling me anything of what had happened they sent their workers to clean it and repair it and to paint it up. The day I was leaving, they came and said, "Mother, we have a small gift for you and for your sick and dying people." Such a beautiful thing!

In Calcutta, also, people are beginning to be very much more charitably minded. In December 1966 some little boys were caught stealing and instead of handing them over to the police they brought them to me. And I asked the children, "But why do you have to do this? Why do you have to do wrong? You are so small." And they said, "Every day, between 4.30 and 7.00 in the evening some big people come and teach us how to steal, and how to do the wrong thing." Then I thought it would be very nice if we could do something for these children to keep them away from those parts at that time. So we started a High School for these street children – boys and girls – to prevent them from being in the streets during those hours. So we are using a school which they close at half past three and we take over at 4.00 because we have not got our own buildings. We take this school from 4.00 to 7.30.

There is a Hindu gentleman, well-to-do, and I told him about the school and so on and he said, "Mother, I will finance the school in memory of my wife." And last year at the closing of the year he came to see the school and he said, "I have never worked so hard in my life as I am working now." And I said, "Why have you to work? You are a millionaire, you have got everything, you don't need to work." And he said, "I work on account of you because the harder I work the more I give you." And it is true because the year before he gave half the amount that he gave this year. So now he is completely involved. And now we have 350 boys and girls between the ages of eleven and eighteen. There are some even of 20 who are kept away from the streets but they are so happy. And there are Brothers who come, and they feed the children before they go to class, for that is the only food they get. So they have a nice hot meal.

One of the teachers in Denmark started child-to-child help, and every child gives a tin of condensed milk every week for a child in India. And so now every child gets one glass of condensed milk and a vitamin tablet every day. Over 1,000 schools in Denmark are involved in this scheme. And we have thousands of children who get a glass of milk every day.

Co-Workers' Newsletter

LOVING COMPASSION

For nearly 800 years Yemen has been closed to the Christian touch. After 800 years our Sisters went there and for the first time the people saw that God really loved them and they call our Sisters "Carriers of God's love". Why? Because they are taking care: they are serving: they are loving. They are putting the love of Christ into a living action and the people say, "It is the first time that we see really Christian love alive . . . alive!" And for them Allah is everything, for every word they say Allah. And they find that those Sisters are able to take care of the lepers, of the dying, of the crippled, of the unwanted; that they are really the people of God, carriers of His love on earth and that their presence in that dark place has lit a new light in the lives of these people.

In all this completely Moslem country, not a sign of Christ. Many people told me, "Don't wear the cross, don't pray the rosary in the street, hide everything." Then I went straight to the Governor and I said, "This is the sign, it's an external sign, but it is a sign that I belong to Him. This is the rosary that we pray and if you can't accept us as we are, then we need not be here." That man said, "You come to bring love into our country. You are the carriers of God's love, you come as you are, and you keep your sign, don't destroy anything."

Pray for us that we may not spoil God's work. And that His work remains His. Let us not use bombs and guns to overcome the world. Let us use love and compassion and we will be able to overcome the whole world and bring Christ's Good News to the world, the news that God loves the world.

Co-Workers' Newsletter

KNOW THE POOR

It seems to me that in England there is a very great need to know who the poor are. I don't think the English are able to recognize their poor. Since they don't know them, they find it hard to love them and even harder to serve them. It would be different if we could have people meet each other face to face. If some English people could take the place of one of our Sisters (just to give you an example) for a while, that would be helpful. If people could get a sense of what it's like to try to find a home for those who are outside dying in the cold, if they could see firsthand how old people are neglected, despised, and abandoned, by nearly everyone, that would be good.

There are people who sleep in the streets of London, people who use makeshift pieces of cardboard and sheets of newspapers to protect themselves. You have people who shiver in the cold and are half frozen in London. No one seems to take the time or the effort to notice these people. The fact that people don't have time for the poor causes the greatest suffering of all. Oh, the terrible loneliness of our elderly living in a small room completely abandoned by family and friends! Not even their neighbours know them by name, nor do they think of even taking them a glass of water. I believe that this is by far the greatest tragedy in the world today. The English should open their hearts to love the poor and lend them a hand by serving them. But they can't do that unless they first know them. Knowledge leads to love and love to service.

One Heart Full of Love
pp. 113–14

THE POVERTY OF LONELINESS

You have a welfare state in England, but I have walked at night and gone into your homes and found people dying unloved. Here you have a different kind of poverty – a poverty of the spirit, of loneliness, and of being unwanted. And that is the worst disease in the world today, not tuberculosis or leprosy. I think England needs more and more for the people to know who the poor are. People in England should give their hearts to love the poor, and also their hands to serve them. And they cannot do that unless they know them, and knowledge will lead them to love, and love to service.

In England and other places, in Calcutta, in Melbourne, in New York, we find lonely people who are known by the number of their room. Why are we not there? Do we really know that there are some people, maybe next door to us? Maybe there is a blind man who would be happy if you would read the newspaper for him; maybe there is a rich person who has no one to visit him – he has plenty of other things, he is nearly drowned in them, but there is not that touch and he needs your touch. Some time back a very rich man came to our place, and he said to me: "Please, either you or somebody, come to my house. I am nearly half-blind and my wife is nearly mental; our children have all gone abroad, and we are dying of loneliness, we are longing for the loving sound of a human voice."

Let us not be satisfied with just giving money. Money is not enough, money can be got, but they need your hearts to love them. So, spread love everywhere you go: first of all in your own home. Give love to your children, to your wife or husband, to a next-door neighbour.

You ask how I should see the task of the Missionaries of Charity if I were a religious Sister or priest in Surrey or Sussex. Well, the task of the Church in such places is much more difficult than what we face in Calcutta, Yemen, or anywhere else, where all the people need is dressing for their wounds, a bowl of rice and a "cuddle", with someone telling them they are loved and wanted. In Surrey and Sussex the problems of your people are deep down, at the bottom of their hearts. They have to come to know you and trust you, to see you as a person with Christ's compassion and love, before their problems will emerge and you can help them. This takes a lot of time! Time for you to be people of prayer and time to give of yourself to each one of your people.

A Gift for God
pp. 75–8

TAKE WHAT YOU NEED

When I went to Tanzania all the non-Christian leaders of the tribes came to me just to thank me for the Sisters. They said they had never seen God's love in action as they saw what the Sisters did for the refugees. More than 12,000 people came at the same time and these little Sisters running in and burying the dead and carrying the sick and all that. It was simply an opening for the whole of that region, for the whole of that Tanzanian people. They had never seen anything like that, so living, so real, and yet so full of joy. The Sisters told me that during that time even the people in the shops would say, "Come Sisters, take what you need, take what you need." And they would go and take from the shops whatever they needed for the people and without paying anything. It was so beautiful, that shows you that the love of Christ in those Sisters infected everybody else. It was the way the Sisters did it, the way they touched the people, the way they carried the dead, the way they buried them.

I will never forget the time when we had terrible floods in Calcutta. A group of the worst kind of Communists were busy at that time killing and shooting and burning and doing all kinds of things. And then when the flood started and we were all walking in water up to our necks, these young men came, thirty of them, and said, "We are at your service, use us." We used to stay until ten o'clock working, but they spent the whole night helping, carrying the people on their heads, and the government couldn't understand that because it was these University students who were doing all the mischief and then they were there like little lambs, doing the most humble work. So the young people are hungry for Christ, they are looking to us to challenge them. You have only to give them a helping hand.

From an address to Co-Workers in the USA 1974

MONEY IS NOT ENOUGH

I remember, when we first came to New York, and Cardinal Cooke wanted to give every Sister five hundred dollars every month. And I looked at him, I said, "Cardinal, do you think God is going to be bankrupt in New York?" He looked at me, thinking, *Maybe she's a little bit off.* He has brought it up again, again, and again, and each time I answered the same way.

When our Sisters went to Paris to begin the work, the church leaders explained about health insurance. They were going to have all the Sisters insured and they had the forms ready.

I said, "No, that is not for us." Everybody was shocked and tried to make me change my mind. "Do the poor that we work with have health insurance?" That settled it.

If we live with the poor, we must share their poverty and depend on the providence of Almighty God for His help. That is our faith.

A Sister was coming to join the Society, and we had not

enough cotton to make a mattress for her, and I told the Sisters, "Take my pillow, I can sleep without a pillow, and finish the mattress." But they refused. So I got up and I took that pillow to them. There was a knock at the gate. The Sister ran down and there was an Englishman with a big cotton mattress. He said, "I'm going to England, I thought Mother Teresa would like to have the mattress."

Living the Word
pp. 34, 35, 97

THE GREATEST SCOURGE

When the Sisters came to Harlem, they began to visit the old people, the shut-ins who often lived alone. They would do the simple things, clean the rooms, wash the clothes.

Once they came to a door and no one answered. The woman had been dead for five days and no one knew – except for the odour in the hallway. So many are known only by the number on the door.

The worst disease today is not leprosy; it is being unwanted, being left out, being forgotten. The greatest scourge is to forget the next person, to be so suffocated, so to say, with things that we have no time for the lonely Jesus – even a person in our own family who needs us.

Maybe if I had not picked up that one person dying on the street, I would not have picked up the thousands. We must think, Ek (Bengali for "One"). I think Ek, Ek. One, One. That is the way to begin.

When his followers deserted Jesus, it was Mary who stayed with him. She remained when He was spat upon, treated like a leper, disowned by all and crucified.

66

Do we remain with our people when they are disowned, thrown out, when they suffer? Do we give them our understanding love? Do we have the eyes of compassion of Mary? Do we understand their pain? Do we recognize their suffering?

Living the Word.
pp. 64–5

IN TUNE WITH GOD

The other day some of the Sisters were telling me that they had gone somewhere (in New York City), and they were told that someone had died in an apartment. No one knew when, and they had to force the door open to get in. What did they find? Rats were eating the body. It was a woman. The Sisters tried to find out who she was, whose daughter or mother or wife. But no one knew anything about that woman except her apartment number. What tremendous poverty! Imagine the loneliness, the feeling of knowing that she was unwanted, despised, and neglected! That is what we as Co-workers must fight in our own families.

We must ask for the grace to love one another. As Jesus said, "Love one another as I have loved you." To be capable of doing that, our Sisters live a life of prayer and sacrifice. That is why we start our day with prayer, Holy Communion, and meditation. Every evening we also have an hour of worship before the Blessed Sacrament. We have permission from our bishop for this time of adoration before the Sacrament. This hour of intimacy with Jesus is something very beautiful. It is the greatest gift that God can give us.

Wherever you find yourself, if you are free and you feel

the need for Jesus, we have daily worship from 6.30 to 7.30 pm in our homes. You are cordially invited to come. Or if it is more practical, go to your own church. Wherever you find yourself, try to begin doing this. Try to put worship into practice in your life. Be alone with Jesus. You will notice a change in your life, in your family, in your parish, and in your environment.

This is something that we should be concerned about as Co-workers. We need to soak up the tender love of Jesus that our people experience when they sense that God loves them. We need to extend to each and every one the assurance that God loves them.

Let's fix our eyes on the cross. What do we see? We see his head bent down to kiss us. Look at his hands. They say ''I love you!'' We see his arms stretched out on the cross as if to embrace us. We see his heart opened wide to receive us. That is the cross, which is represented by the crucifix that most of us have in our homes. Each time we glance at it, it should help us to fall in love with Christ. It should help us to love Him with sincerity of heart. What greater love is there than God's love for each one of us? His love isn't a fantasy. It is real.

Strive to soak up the simplicity and purity of Christ. Try to be more in tune with God and more open to him, so that you will be able to see his face. Jesus said, ''Blessed are the pure of heart, for they will see God.'' We need to have an open heart to be able to see God in others. Let's pray for the grace we need. Pray for us so that we may be able to accomplish God's work with plenty of love. Pray for us that we won't spoil it. Pray that you and I may really be one. I consider you as our co-workers, an integral part of us, a very intimate part of our congregation.

One Heart Full of Love
pp. 94–6

A SIGN OF HIS LOVE

Thousands of people suffering from AIDS walk the streets.

I opened our first house for AIDS patients in New York City. Already fourteen are dead because there is no cure for this disease.

One patient had to leave our home to go to hospital. When I visited him, he said to me, "Mother Teresa, you are my friend. I want to talk to you alone."

What did he say after twenty-five years of being away from God? "When I get the terrible pain in my head, I share it with Jesus and suffer as He did when He was crowned with thorns. When I get the terrible pain in my back, I share it with Him when He was scourged at the pillar, and when I get the pain in my hands and feet, I share it with Him when He was nailed to the cross. I ask you to take me home. I want to die with you."

I got permission and took him to our home, Gift of Love, and took him into the chapel. I never heard anyone talk to Jesus like this man talked to Him, so tenderly, so full of love. Three days later he died.

Prayer enlarges the heart until it is capable of containing God's gift of Himself. Ask and seek and your heart will grow big enough to receive Him and keep Him as your own.

Co-Workers' Newsletter

SMILE OF LOVE

Some weeks back one of our Brothers came to me in anguish and said, "My calling is to work for the lepers." He really loved the lepers. "I want to devote my life, my whole being, to carry out that calling," he said.

I replied, "You are mistaken, Brother. Your calling is to belong to Jesus. He has chosen you for Himself, and work is only a means of love for Him in action. So the work you carry out is of no importance. What is important is that you belong to Him, that you are His, that He gives you the means to do what you have to do."

The same is true for us: it does not matter what we do or where we are, as long as we bear in mind that we are His possessions, that Jesus can do with us whatever He wants, that we owe Him our love, and that we love Him. Whether we work for the rich or on behalf of the poor, whether we work among people of high society or among inhabitants of the inner city, what is important is only the love we put into carrying out our job.

Maybe you and I are the only ones through whom Jesus can come to those whom we are touching. Because in the rich, it is not that we love the preciousness of their gifts but that our love addresses the person who belongs to God, the child of God who is our brother and our sister.

Therefore, let us try to spread this love of Christ – above all in our own family, among our own, my husband, my wife, my children. Does my home, my community, burn in love? Do I have time to devote to my Sisters? Do I have time for my children, for my husband, for my wife?

I cannot forget my mother. She was usually very busy all day long. But when sunset drew near, it was her custom to hurry with her tasks in order to be ready to receive my father. At the time we did not understand, and we would smile and even joke a little about it. Today I cannot help but call to mind that great delicacy of love that she had for him. No matter what happened, she was always prepared, with a smile on her lips, to welcome him.

Today we have no time. Fathers and mothers are so busy that when children come home they are not welcomed with love or with a smile.

This is really what Jesus asks us to do: to love each other as the Father has loved Him. And how did the Father love Christ? Through sacrifice: He delivered Him to death for our salvation.

We have to love Christ to the point of hurting. I do not want you to give your surplus. I want you to sacrifice something you love, like that child I have mentioned in other circumstances who deprived himself of sugar in order to give it to our orphans. It was a great gesture for such a small child to love to the point of depriving himself of something.

Remember us in your prayers, so that we will be able to be united with Christ through prayer and sacrifice. This is the ideal of the young sisters who embrace the life of our congregation, something which is really very beautiful. We want to undertake a life of poverty, of prayer, and of sacrifice that will lead us to the service of the poor.

Pray also for your children, that Christ's calling and choice may rest upon your families for a vocation to the priesthood or to religious life. It is a gift from God to a family.

Heart of Joy
pp. 104–6 and 109

GOD IS THE SOURCE

All those who have witnessed our work, have been able to see that God is the source. Just as Jesus said, "when men see your good deeds, they will give praise to your Father who is in heaven."

This is one of the reasons why I accept the distinctions and honours that are continually being bestowed on me from one place or another . . . They don't affect me deeply. It is something that comes with our work, but it doesn't *stop with me*. When an honour is bestowed, it isn't just for me.

I am sure that what just happened at Cambridge when I received an honorary degree wasn't intended simply for me. Personally I felt like a small, weak child surrounded by an immense crowd of poor from everywhere. By bestowing an honour on me, they bestowed it also on you, on each of the Sisters, and on each of the poor. Those at that great University know that every act of love must be shared, that you and I depend upon and support one another in our work. They also know that we are aware of the plight of the poor in the world, that we consider them our brothers and sisters. This is what makes many fall to their knees and encourages them to accept their brothers and sisters in the poor. That is why I showed my gratitude. Thinking of you and in the name of all of you, I said, "I accept." Otherwise the honour would have no meaning. I said at Cambridge when I addressed those who had assembled: "You know full well that I have not studied theology. I just simply try always to live it out." I wanted to make it clear that I was unqualified for what the academic world calls an honorary degree as a Doctor of Divinity.

In reality, the event was a gift from God. And it was not just for me personally but for you, for the Sisters and for our poor. We must appreciate and accept it with all humility of heart, so that we can offer it to Jesus. After all, it belongs to Him. All glory and honour are His.

One Heart Full of Love
pp. 66–7

SANCTITY IS SIMPLE

People say clever things, big things, beautiful things, wonderful things, but I say stupid things, things that little children can understand and yet people are hungry for something like that, something they can make their own, because sanctity is not a luxury of the few. Sanctity is a simple duty for you and for me, and sanctity, what is sanctity? Sanctity is the acceptance of the will of God with a big smile . . . that's all. Just that acceptance, to accept Him as He comes in our life, accepting to take from us what He wants, to make use of us as He wants, to put us where He wants, to use us as He wants . . . without consulting us. But we like to be consulted. And for Him to use us, to make use of us, to break us to pieces and yet let every single piece be only His, to empty us completely. That acceptance is to be empty, that acceptance is to be broken in pieces, that acceptance is to succeed and to fail, to be in the public eye.

I believe yesterday that I was the first citizen of . . . where was I yesterday . . . ? And I said thank you very much but I don't understand what it means. It makes no difference, it is coming from the same hand and tomorrow if people would say "Crucify", all right, it is the same loving hand. That acceptance for you and for me, it is what Jesus wants from us. To allow Him to use us . . . without consulting us. This is the work of the vine and the branch. I think you and

I have a very big responsibility in the world today. It doesn't matter what people say or think, that's the least thing, it does not bother us.

Let us again look back into our own homes . . . what is the love of God in my home, in my community. I find it sometimes much easier to smile at the people outside than to smile at my Sisters. I find it difficult sometimes to smile at them, and quite possibly the same thing happens to you, so let us bring that burning love into our homes.

From an address to Co-Workers

CONVERSION OF HEART

Oh, I hope I am converting. I don't mean what you think. I hope we are converting hearts. Not even Almighty God can convert a person unless that person wants it. What we are all trying to do by our work, by serving the people, is to come closer to God. If in coming face to face with God we accept Him in our lives, then we are converting. We become a better Hindu, a better Muslim, a better Catholic, a better whatever we are, and then by being better we come closer and closer to Him. If we accept Him fully in our lives, then that is conversion. What approach would I use? For me, naturally, it would be a Catholic one, for you it may be Hindu, for someone else, Buddhist, according to each one's conscience. What God is in your mind you must accept. But I cannot prevent myself from trying to give you what I have.

I am not afraid to say I am in love with Jesus because He is everything to me. But you may have a different picture in your life. And this is the way that conversion has to be understood – people think that conversion is just changing overnight. It is not like that. Nobody, not even your father or your mother, can make you do that. Not even Almighty God can force a person. Even Jesus, though He was God Himself, could not convert the hearts of the people unless they allowed Him to.

I want very much for people to come to know God, to love Him, to serve Him, for that is true happiness. And what I have I want everyone in the world to have. But it is their choice. If they have seen the light they can follow it. I cannot give them the light: I can only give the means. If I go into Kalighat and do some work there and really serve the people with great love and sacrifice, then naturally they will begin to think of God. Once they think, they will come to know, and knowing, they will want to love, and if they love they will want to serve.

There are many Hindu ladies who want our way of life, the life of poverty, prayer, sacrifice and service. They want the life of a missionary. But they wish to retain their faith, their own belief in God. Now I don't know how this works – you see, they want to take vows, they want prayer, they want complete dedication. I am trying to think of a way.

Mother Teresa: Her People and Her Work
pp. 136–7

LET GOD USE YOU

What we allow God to use us for, that is important. What He is doing through us, that is important. Because we are religious and our vocation is not to work for the lepers or the dying, our vocation is to belong to Jesus. Because I belong to Him, the work is a means for me to put my love for Him into action. So it is not an end, it is a means. Because my vocation is to belong to God properly, love Him with undivided love and chastity, I take the vows.

I see Christ in every person I touch because He has said, "I was hungry, I was thirsty, I was naked, I was sick, I was suffering, I was homeless and you took me . . ." It is as simple as that. Every time I give a piece of bread, I give it to Him. That is why we must find a hungry one, and a naked one. That is why we are totally bound to the poor.

The vows we take make our religious life. Our vow of chastity is nothing but our undivided love for Christ in chastity, then we proceed to the freedom of poverty – poverty is nothing but freedom. And that total surrender is obedience. If I belong to God, if I belong to Christ, then He must be able to use me. That is obedience. Then we give wholehearted service to the poor. That is service. They complete each other. That is our life.

If you really belong to the work that has been entrusted to you, then you must do it with your whole heart. And you can bring salvation only by being honest and by really working with God. It is not how much we are doing but how much love, how much honesty, how much faith, is put into doing it. It makes no difference what we are doing. What you are doing, I cannot do, and what I am doing, you cannot do. But all of us are doing what God has given us to do. Only sometimes we forget and we spend more time looking at somebody else and wishing we were doing something else.

We waste our time thinking of tomorrow and today we let the day pass and yesterday is gone.

Mother Teresa: Her People and Her Work
pp. 137–8

THIRSTING FOR PEACE

We shall make this year a year of peace in a particular way – to be able to do this we shall try to talk more to God and with God and less with men and to men. Let us preach the peace of Christ like He did. He went about doing good; He did not stop His works of charity because the Pharisees and others hated Him or tried to spoil His Father's work. He just went about doing good. Cardinal Newman wrote: "Help me to spread thy fragrance everywhere I go – let me preach thee without preaching, not by words but by my example – by the sympathetic influence of what I do, the evident fullness of the love my heart bears to thee." Our works of love are nothing but works of peace. Let us do them with greater love and efficiency – each in her own or his own work in daily life; in your home – in your neighbour. It is always the same Christ who says:

I was hungry – not only for food, but for peace that comes from a pure heart.

I was thirsty – not for water, but for peace that satiates the passionate thirst of passion for war.

I was naked – not for clothes, but for that beautiful dignity of men and women for their bodies.

I was homeless – not for a shelter made of bricks, but for a heart that understands, that covers, that loves.

This year let us be this to Christ in our neighbour wherever the Missionaries of Charity and their Co-Workers be. Let us radiate the peace of God and so light His light and extinguish in the world and in the hearts of all men all hatred, and love for power. Let the Missionaries of Charity and the Co-Workers, in every country wherever they are, meet God with a smile – everywhere they go in everyone.

Something Beautiful for God
pp. 72–3

ONE WITH CHRIST

We need to pray to be able to be so one with Christ, one with God that nothing will separate us from the love of Christ, that oneness. For the fruit of prayer is the deepening of faith, and the fruit of faith is love, and the fruit of love is service. So to be a Co-Worker you must know how to pray. Not big prayers, but the prayer of the child, an open heart, a humble heart.

"Learn," Jesus said, "Learn of me because I am meek and humble of heart." He didn't ask us to learn big things. He asked us to learn from Him to be meek and humble of heart. And it is so beautiful to think that He puts meekness first: meekness with one another, meekness that means love in action, that kindness, that thoughtfulness. And Jesus said, "By this they will know that you are my disciples." By this meekness, by this kindness, people will know that you are a Co-Worker, that you are there to radiate joy, to radiate love and meekness. And then He says, humility, humility with God. The child of God.

And it is, I think, a privilege for us to have been chosen. He has called you by your name; each one of you has been called by your name. You belong to Him in a special way. You are precious to Him because He loves you. And He has put love into your hearts for you to be able to give that love to others. You must not be afraid to love, and to love until it hurts.

But love begins at home. You must make your home the centre of burning love. The sunshine of God's love must be in your home first. You must be that hope of eternal happiness to your husband, to your wife, to your child, to your grandfather, grandmother, to whoever is connected with you. You are a worker in a big firm, you are a Co-Worker, but you don't even know your people. You have to be the burning flame of God's love to the people who are working with you, who are working for you. Can they look up and see the joy of loving in your face? Can they look up and see the joy of a clean heart? Can they look up and see Jesus in you? This is very important for a Co-Worker. And how do we reach to that if not by prayer? Maybe not big prayers, but talk from the heart to God. Open your heart to God.

Most of you have learned to pray from babyhood, you have learned to pray in your families. Teach. Today we have so many difficulties with the young people. And yet the young people are hungry for God. They're hungry to give all to God. But they are misled. And it is you, as Co-Workers, you must be that burning flame of love there. That's the joy of loving God, the joy of loving God in your neighbour. That's a true Co-Worker. I don't believe in meetings, big meetings, big things like that. That's not necessary for the Co-Worker. If the mother has to cook the food for her husband and children, that comes first. If you have to wash the napkins of the baby, that comes first. If the husband has to go to do some special work, that comes first. That comes first. Family comes first. The home of the Co-Worker must be another Nazareth. Love. Joy. Peace. Unity. Then you will be able to give to others.

From an address to Co-Workers

REJOICE IN THE LORD

Joy was the password of the first Christians. St Paul, how often he repeats himself, "Rejoice in the Lord always, again I say to you rejoice." In return for the great grace of baptism, the priest tells the newly baptized, "May you serve the Church joyfully."

Joy is not simply a matter of temperament. In the service of God and souls, it is always hard: all the more reason why we should try to acquire it and make it grow in our hearts.

. . . Joy is prayer – joy is strength – joy is love – joy is a net of love by which you can catch souls. God loves a cheerful giver. She gives most who gives with joy. The best way to show our gratitude to God and the people is to accept everything with joy. A joyful heart is the normal result of a heart burning with love . . . Never let anything so fill you with sorrow as to make you forget the joy of Christ Risen. We all long for Heaven where God is, but we have it in our power to be in Heaven with Him right now – to be happy with Him at this very moment. But being happy with Him now means loving as He loves, helping as He helps, giving as He gives, serving as He serves, rescuing as He rescues, being with Him twenty-four hours a day, touching Him in His distressing disguise.

Sadness is like gangrene that eats up the very bone. Sad religious are the greatest stumbling block to vocations because young people, like God, love a cheerful giver.

From an address to Co-Workers

THE LEAST OF MY BROTHERS

At the hour of death Christ is going to judge us; what we have done to the poor? What we have been to the poor? "I was hungry and you did not give me to eat", hungry for love, hungry for bread, hungry for justice, hungry for that human dignity and you passed me by. And naked, naked for that respect, for justice, for acknowledging that he too is one of us – created by the same loving hand of God, to love and to be loved. Homeless through sheer loneliness: the shut-ins: the unwanted, the unloved; the uncared for; the leper; the blind; the lame; where are they? Do I know them? Do I know the poor of my own home first? Do I know that maybe in my own home, in my own community, there may be somebody who is feeling very lonely, very unwanted, very handicapped? Do I know that? Maybe my husband, my wife, my child is lonely in my own home. Do I know that? Where are the old people today? They are put in institutions. Why? Because they are unwanted, they are a burden. I remember, some time ago I visited a very wonderful home for the old people and there it was; they had everything and there were about forty there. They were all looking towards the door: There was not a smile on their faces and I asked the Sister in charge of them. I said, "Sister, why are these people not smiling? Why are they always looking towards the door?" And she, very beautifully had to answer and give the truth. "This is every day; they are longing for somebody to come and visit them. They are always looking. 'Maybe my son, maybe my daughter, maybe somebody will come and visit me.' " This is great poverty and I remember also, once I picked up a woman from a dustbin and I knew she was dying. I took her out and took her to the convent. She kept on saying, repeating the same words, "My son did this to me." Not once did she utter the words "I'm hungry", "I'm dying", "I'm suffering". But she kept on repeating, "My son did this to me." It took me a long time to help her to say: "I forgive my son" before she died, a long time. This is poverty.

From an address in Malta to the
World Congress of the Lasallion Federation.
August 1976

THE BREAD OF LIFE

Jesus made himself into the bread of life to be able to satisfy our hunger for God, our love for God. And then to satisfy His own hunger for our love, He made Himself the hungry one, the naked one, the homeless one, and He said, "When you did this to the least of my brethren, you did it to me." We are contemplatives right in the middle of the world, because we are touching Christ twenty-four hours a day. Our eucharistic union with Christ has to produce that fruit because Jesus has said, "I am the vine and you are the branch" and on the branch we get the fruit, not on the vine, so what a tremendous responsibility for you and for me, for all of us, that the fruit will depend on the union of the branch with the vine. That is why it is necessary that our union with Christ must be something real, not in imagination, but something living, something with conviction. And that has to come from our own homes first, and if we don't love our own family from within, and our neighbours, then we are living a big failure – nobody loves alone. Your vocation is that Christ has chosen you. Why you and not others? Why me and not others? I don't know – it is a mystery. Being together should help us to deepen our love for Jesus, to deepen our knowledge of God, and that knowledge will lead us to love Him, and love will lead us to serve Him.

Jesus has said, "I was hungry, I was naked, I was homeless." We must attend to our own children first, to our own families, and others. There is much suffering in the world – very much. Suffering from hunger, from homelessness, from all kinds of diseases. But I still think the greatest suffering is being lonely, being unwanted, being unloved, just having no one, having forgotten what it is to have the human touch, human love, what it is to be wanted, what it is to be loved, what it is to have your own people. I think this can be found even in the rich families. And this is why I say again that we must bring our mission of love and compassion to our own homes first. To be able to do that we need prayer and sacrifice. Some time ago forty professors from the United States came to our house in Calcutta. We talked and then one of them asked me, "Tell us something that will help us change our lives." And I said to them, "Smile at each other, make time for each other, enjoy each other." And then one of them asked me, "Are you married?" I said, "Yes, and sometimes I find it very difficult to smile at Jesus!" I think they understood very well. Jesus can be very demanding sometimes.

From a meeting of Co-Workers,
Germany, August 1976

THE JOY OF LOVING

When Mary visited St Elizabeth something very strange happened – the little unborn child leaped with joy in his mother's womb. How strange that God used the little unborn child to be the first to welcome God made man.

Now, there is abortion and the little child, made in the image of God, is destroyed. That little one, in the womb of his mother, has been created for the same great aim – to love and to be loved. So today, when we are together, just for one moment, thank our parents for wanting us, for giving us the wonderful gift of life, the opportunity to live, to love and to be loved. Jesus spent most of His time repeating the same thing – "Love one another as God loves you. As the Father has loved me, I love you. Love one another." When we look at the cross we know how much Jesus loved us. When we look at the tabernacle we know how much He loves us now.

Now that is why it is very important to pray if we really want to love and be loved. Let us learn to pray, Let us teach our children to pray, and pray with them, for the fruit of prayer is faith – "I believe" –, and the fruit of faith is love, – "I love" – the fruit of love is service, "I serve," and the fruit of service is peace. Where does this love, this peace begin? In our own family . . .

And so today let us pray, let us pray, for prayer will give us a clean heart and a clean heart can see the face of God even in that little unborn child. It is really a gift of God, prayer, because it gives us the joy of loving, the joy of sharing, the joy of keeping our family together. Pray and bring your children to pray with you. I *feel* all the terrible things that are happening today. I always say that if a mother can kill her own child what is left for others – to kill each other! God himself says, "Even if a mother could forget her child I will not forget you. I have carved you on the palm of my hand, you are precious to me, I love you." God's own words, "I love you."

From an address to the International Congress on Family Life
Paris 1986

WHO IS JESUS TO ME?

the Word made flesh.
the Bread of Life.
the Victim offered for our sins on the cross.
the Sacrifice offered at the Holy Mass for the sins of
 the world and mine.
the Word — to be spoken.
the Truth — to be told.
the Way — to be walked.
the Light — to be lit.
the Life — to be lived.
the Love — to be loved.
the Joy — to be shared.
the Sacrifice — to be offered.
the Peace — to be given.
the Bread of Life — to be eaten.
the Hungry — to be fed.
the Thirsty — to be satiated.
the Naked — to be clothed.
the Homeless — to be taken in.
the Sick — to be healed.
the Lonely — to be loved.
the Unwanted — to be wanted.
the Leper — to wash his wounds.
the Beggar — to give him a smile.
the Drunkard — to listen to him.
the Mentally ill — to be protected.
the Little One — to embrace him.
the Blind — to lead him.
the Dumb — to speak for him.
the Crippled — to walk with him.
the Drug Addict — to befriend him.
the Prostitute — to remove from danger and befriend her.

the Prisoner – to be visited.
the Old – to be served.

To me Jesus is my God
      Jesus is my Spouse
      Jesus is my Life
      Jesus is my only Love
      Jesus is my all in all
      Jesus is my Everything.

Jesus, I love with my whole heart, with my whole being. I have given Him all, even my sins, and He has espoused me to Himself in tenderness and love. Now and for life I am the Spouse of my Crucified Spouse. Amen.

(Meditation of Mother Teresa, in hospital
June 19, 1983)

PRAY FOR THE PATIENT

Yours is not just a profession – yours is a vocation. It's a consecrated life – because in touching the sick, in healing the sick, Jesus said: "You did it to me". How full of love your hearts must be – to be able to love like Jesus. Because the sick, the lonely, the disabled come to you with hope and that is why they must be able to receive from you that tender love, that compassion.

The sick and suffering don't need pity and sympathy; they need love and compassion. That's why it's very important for you to realize the words of Christ, "You did it to me". At the hour of death we are going to be judged on what we have been to Him in the poor; "I was sick, I was hungry, I was naked, I was homeless and you did it to me."

Where does this love begin? In your own home. Love begins at home. And how do we begin to love? In the family; by praying together. Because the family that prays together, stays together. And if you stay together, you will love one another as Jesus loves you.

You cannot love the patients and the suffering if you have no love for your own at home.

It is nearly impossible to bring that presence of Christ to the suffering if you do not learn to love at home. That is why it is very necesary for us to pray. Because the fruit of prayer is deepening of faith. And the fruit of faith is love. And the fruit of love is service. Because prayer gives a clean heart and a clean heart can see God. And if we see God in each other then we will love one another. And if we see God in each other then we will love each other as Jesus loves us. This is all that Jesus came on earth to teach us – to love one another.

Before you touch a patient, before you listen to the patient – PRAY. Because you need a clean heart to love that patient. And you need clean hands to touch that patient. Today medical work has become a business. That's why I'm very happy to see you; that you come here and share the joy of loving with the Sisters. It is not how much we do – it is how much love we put into the doing. That's why I'm very, very grateful to each one of you for coming and sharing this joy of loving Jesus in the suffering.

I will pray for you that, through this work of your hands and hearts, you may grow in holiness. Holiness is not the luxury of the few! it's a simply duty for you and for me . . . Whatever you are doing to the sick and suffering you are doing it to Jesus.

Translation of a speech to Gemelli hospital doctors in Rome 1983

ALL TALK?

Some people talk about hunger, but they don't come and say, "Mother, here are five rupees. Buy food for these people." But they can give a most beautiful lecture on hunger.

I had the most extraordinary experience once in Bombay. There was a big conference about hunger. I was supposed to go to that meeting and I lost the way. Suddenly I came to that place, and right in front of the door to where hundreds of people were talking about food and hunger, I found a dying man.

I took him out and I took him home.

He died there.

He died of hunger.

And the people inside were talking about how in fifteen years we will have so much food, so much this, so much that, and that man died.

See the difference?

I never look at the masses as my responsibility.

I look at the individual. I can love only one person at a time. I can feed only one person at a time.

Just one, one, one.

You get closer to Christ by coming closer to each other. As Jesus said, "Whatever you do to the least of my brethren, you do to me."

So you begin . . . I begin.

I picked up one person.

Maybe if I hadn't picked up that one person I wouldn't have picked up 42,000. The whole work is only a drop in the ocean. But if I didn't put the drop in, the ocean would be one drop less.

Same thing for you.

Same thing in your family.

Same thing in the church where you go.
Just begin . . . one, one, one.
At the end of life we will not be judged by
    how many diplomas we have received
    how much money we have made
    how many great things we have done;
We will be judged by
    "I was hungry and you gave me to eat
    I was naked and you clothed me
    I was homeless and you took me in."
Hungry not only for bread – but hungry for love
Naked not only for clothing – but naked of human dignity and respect.
Homeless not only for want of a room of bricks – but homeless because of rejection.
This is Christ in distressing disguise.

Co-Workers' Newsletter
1987

LOVE BEGINS AT HOME

Every child has been created for greater things, to love and be loved, in the image of God. That's why people must decide beforehand if they really want to have a child. Once a child is conceived, there is life, God's life. That child has a right to live and be cared for. Abortion destroys two lives, the life of the child and the conscience of the mother. It's not only destroying. It's killing. It is a child of God, no? Created for greater things, just like you and me.

Many of the troubles of modern society are caused by

broken families. Many mothers and fathers are so busy that they are never at home.

Children come home from school and there is no one
to receive them
to pay attention to them
to encourage them if they are sad
to share their joy if they are happy.
Children long for somebody
to accept them
to love them
to praise them
to be proud of them.

If they do not have this, they will go to the streets where there are plenty of people to accept them. The child can be lost. Much hatred and destruction is caused when a child is lost to the family.

Like Our Lady and St Joseph we must go and search for the child. When Jesus was lost they went and searched. They did not sit and wait. They did not rest until they found him.

We must bring the child back, make the child feel wanted. Without the child there is no hope.

Love begins at home. If we do not love one another whom we see all day how can we love those we see only once?

We show love by thoughtfulness
by kindness
by sharing joy
by sharing a smile . . .
Through the little things.

A little child has no difficulty in loving, . . . has no obstacles to love. And that is why Jesus said: ''Unless you become like little children''.

Co-Workers' Newsletter
1988

DREAM BIG, ACT S

Be caring, quick to notice and to respond to
Maybe just carrying a bucket of water, ma
fulness at table.

Be a bridge-builder. Listen to and respect th   ...on of
others allowing them to have their full say.

Be generous but discreet in your actions, giving of your
best. A quiet doer is better than a noisy complainer.

Be a peacemaker. Heal broken relationships. Smile five
times a day at someone you do not really wish to smile
at.

Be able to stand up for your own beliefs. Remain the same
kind of person at home, school, church even if these beliefs
make you unpopular.

Be conscious of social injustices but do not try to change
the whole world at one go. Feed one hungry neighbour
instead of lamenting on world hunger.

Be faithful to your daily commitments: studies, prayer,
work. Maintain your promises to visit your sick neighbour.

Be willing to accept your weakness and failures without anger and frustration. Give yourself fully to God.
He will use you to accomplish great things on condition
that you believe more in His love than in your own
weakness.

Co-Workers' Newsletter
1987

NO TIME?

In His passion Jesus taught us how to forgive out of love, how to forget out of humility. So let us examine our hearts and see if there is any unforgiven hurt − any unforgotten bitterness! The quickest and surest way is the tongue − use it for the good of others. If you think well of others, you will also speak well of others and to others. From the abundance of the heart the mouth speaketh. If your heart is full of love, you will speak of love. If you forgive others the wrong they have done, your heavenly Father will also forgive you; but if you do not forgive others, then the wrongs you have done will not be forgiven by your Father. It is easy to love those who are far away. It isn't always easy to love those who are right next to us. It is easier to offer a dish of rice to satisfy the hunger of a poor person than to fill up the loneliness and suffering of someone lacking love in our own family.

I think today the world is upside down, and is suffering so much because there is so very little love in the home, and in family life. We have no time for our children, we have no time for each other, there is no time to enjoy each other.

Love begins at home; love lives in homes, and that is why there is so much suffering and so much unhappiness in the world today . . .

Everybody today seems to be in such a terrible rush, anxious for greater developments and greater riches and so on, so that children have very little time for their parents. Parents have very little time for each other, and in the home begins the disruption of the peace of the world.

People who really love each other fully and truly − they are the happiest people in the world, and we see that with our very poor people. They love their children, and they love their home. They may have very little, they may have nothing, but they are happy people . . .

Jesus did not say: "Love the whole world," but He said: "Love one another!" You can only love one person at a time. If you look at the numbers, you get lost, and while you are talking about hunger, somebody is dying next to you . . . If you want to do something beautiful for God, you should be looking for the poor around you.

Co-Workers' Newsletter
1986

TAKE UP YOUR CROSS

Jesus said to the young people of His time: "If you want to be my disciples take up the cross and follow me". Before He took His own cross, He knew that we needed Him.

He made himself into the bread of life and He said: "Unless you eat my flesh and drink my blood you cannot live, you cannot follow me. You cannot be my disciples".

Today in you and in me, in the young of the world, He relives his passion. He relives it in the young child, the hungry child, who eats the piece of bread crumb by crumb because she is afraid lest the bread will finish and she will be hungry again.

Do I see that? Very often we look and we do not see. We all have to take the cross, we all have to follow Christ to Calvary, if we want to rise with Him. And I think that's why Jesus, before He died, gave us His body, gave us His blood that we may live, that we may have the courage, that we may have life to be able to carry the cross and follow Him, step by step.

We see Jesus. Are we there to help Him? Are we there with our sacrifice, with our bread, real bread? There are thousands of people who die for a piece of bread. There are thousands and thousands of people who die for a little bit of love, for a little bit of recognition . . .

Are we a mother to the suffering? A mother of love, of understanding? Are we there to understand our young people when they fall, when they are lonely, when they feel unwanted? Are we there?

Simon of Cyrene took up the cross and followed Jesus, helped Jesus to carry His cross. And Veronica. Are we a Veronica to our poor? To the lonely ones, to the unwanted ones? Are we there to wipe away the sorrow? Are we there to share their suffering? Are we there? Or are we the proud who pass by, who look and can't see.

How many times we have picked up people from the street who have lived like animals and long to die like angels. Are we there to lift them up? Do you see people sitting in the park, very lonely, unwanted, uncared for, so miserable? We pass the word, they are alcoholics. I don't care. That is Jesus who needs your hand to wipe that face. Are you there to do it or do you pass by?

Jesus fell for you and for me. He was stripped of His clothes. Today the little one before its birth is stripped of love. It must die because we don't want that child. That child must go naked because we don't want him and Jesus accepted that terrible suffering. That unborn child accepts that terrible suffering because it has no choice. But I have choice to want him, to love him, to keep him. My brother, my sister.

Jesus Crucified. How many handicapped people, mentally retarded, young people fill the hospitals? How many are there in our own homes? Do we ever visit them? Do we ever go to share with them that Crucifixion? Jesus said, If you want to be my disciples take the cross and follow me. And

MY BROTHER, MY SISTER

I think God wants to prove His greatness by using nothingness. In spite of all our defects, God is in love with us and keeps using you and me to light the light of love and compassion in the world.

Each time Jesus wanted to prove His love for us He was rejected by humanity. Before His birth His parents asked for a simple dwelling place and there was none because His parents were poor and there was nowhere. The innkeeper looked at the dress of Joseph the carpenter – thinking that he would be unable to pay, he was refused. But Mother Earth opened its cave and took in the Son of God.

Again, before the Redemption and the Resurrection, He was rejected by His people. They did not want Him; they wanted Caesar. They did not want Him; they wanted Barabbas. At the end, it was as if His own Father did not want Him either because He was covered with our sins, for in His loneliness He cried out, "My God, my God, why hast thou forsaken me?"

Yesterday is always today with God. Therefore today in the world Jesus stands covered with our sins in the distressing disguise of my Sister, my Brother. Do I want Him?

In each of our lives, Jesus comes as bread of life to be eaten – to be consumed by us. This is how He loves us. Jesus comes in our human life as the hungry one, the other, hoping to be fed with the bread of our lives, our hearts, our hands. In loving and serving we prove that we have been created in the image and likeness of God: for God is love and when we love we are like God. This is what Jesus meant when He said, "Be you perfect as your heavenly father is perfect."

Unpublished

THE BEAUTY OF OUR HEARTS

Humility is truth; therefore in all sincerity we must be able to look up and say, "I can do all things in Him who strengthens me." Because of this assertion of St Paul's, you must have a certain confidence in doing your work, or rather God's work, well, efficiently, even perfectly: with Jesus and for Jesus. Be also convinced that by yourself you can do nothing, have nothing, but sin, weakness and misery: that all the gifts of nature and of grace which you have, you have from God.

It is beautiful to see the humility of Christ, "Who being in the form of God thought it not robbery to be equal with God. But emptied himself, taking the form of a servant, being made in the likeness of man".

This humility of Jesus can be seen in the crib, in the exile in Egypt, in the hidden life, in the inability to make people understand Him, in the desertion of His apostles, in the hatred of the Jews and all the terrible sufferings and death of His Passion; and now in His permanent state of humility in the tabernacle where He has reduced Himself to such a small particle of bread that the priest can hold Him with his two fingers. The more we empty ourselves, the more room we give God to fill.

Let us beg of Our Lady to make our hearts meek and humble like her son's heart. It was from her and in her that the heart of Jesus was formed. Let us try to pray again and again for humility and meekness. We learn humility through accepting humiliations cheerfully. Do not let a chance pass by. It is so very easy to be proud and harsh, moody and selfish – so easy, but we have been created for greater things. Why stoop down to things that will spoil the beauty of our hearts?

Unpublished

98

BE STILL

God is the friend of silence. His language is silence. "Be still and know that I am God". He requires us to be silent to discover Him. In the silence of the heart He speaks to us.

Jesus spent forty days in silence before beginning His public life. He often retired alone, spent the night on the mountain in silence and prayer. He who spoke with authority spent His early life in silence.

The Word of God is speechless today – in the Eucharist His silence is the highest and the truest praise of the Father. It is the Adoration of God. We need silence to be alone with God, to speak to Him, to ponder His words deep in our hearts. We need to be alone with God in silence to be renewed and to be transformed. Silence gives us a new outlook on life. In it we are filled with the energy of God Himself that makes us do all things with joy. Silence is at the root of our union with God and with one another.

The fruit of silence is prayer,
The fruit of prayer is faith,
The fruit of faith is love and
The fruit of love is silence.

Unpublished

NICODEMUS

I think, dear friend, I understand you better now. I am afraid I could not answer to your deep suffering. I don't know why, but you to me are like Nicodemus, and I am sure the

answer is the same — "Unless you become a little child . . ."
I am sure you will understand beautifully everything — if
you would only become a little child in God's hands. Your
longing for God is so deep, and yet he keeps Himself away
from you. He must be forcing Himself to do so, because He
loves you so much as to give Jesus to die for you and for
me. Christ is longing to be your food. Surrounded with
fullness of living food, you allow yourself to starve. The
personal love Christ has for you is infinite — the small
difficulty you have regarding the Church is finite. Overcome
the finite with the infinite. Christ created you because He
wanted you. I know what you feel — terrible longing, with
dark emptiness — and yet, He is the one in love with you.
I do not know if you have seen these few lines before, but
they fill and empty me:

My God, my God, what is a heart
That thou should'st so eye and woo,
Pouring upon it all thy heart
As if thou hadst nothing else to do?

Mother Teresa writing to Malcolm Muggeridge

TOUCHING THE BODY OF CHRIST

We picked up a young man from the streets of Calcutta. He
was very highly educated and had many degrees. He had
fallen into bad hands and had his passport stolen. After
some time I asked him why he had left home. He said his
father did not want him. "From childhood he never looked
me in the eyes. He became jealous of me, so I left home."
After much praying, the Sisters helped him to return home,

100

to forgive his father, and this has helped both of them. This is a case of very great poverty.

Our Sisters and Brothers work for the poorest of the poor, who aren't wanted, aren't loved, are sick and die, for the lepers and the little children, but I can tell you I have never yet in these twenty-five years heard a poor person grumble or curse or feel miserable. I remember I picked up a person from the street who was nearly eaten up with maggots, and he said: "I have lived like an animal in the street but I am going to die like an angel, loved and cared for." And he did die like an angel – a very beautiful death.

We have a rule that the very next day new arrivals must go to the Home for the Dying. So I told a girl who had come from outside India to join the Missionaries of Charity, "You saw Father during Holy Mass, with what love and care he touched Jesus in the Host. Do the same when you go to the Home for the Dying, because it is the same Jesus you will find there in the broken bodies of our poor." After three hours the newcomer came back and said to me with a big smile – I have never seen a smile quite like that – "Mother, I have been touching the body of Christ for three hours." And I said to her: "How – what did you do?" She replied: "When we arrived there, they brought a man who had fallen into a drain, and been there for some time. He was covered with wounds and dirt and maggots, and I cleaned him and I knew I was touching the body of Christ."

A Gift for God
pp. 66–9

101

NOT FOR A THOUSAND POUNDS

There must be a reason why some people can afford to live well. They must have worked for it. I only feel angry when I see waste. When I see people throwing away things that we could use.

The trouble is that rich people, well-to-do people, very often don't really know who the poor are; and that is why we can forgive them, for knowledge can only lead to love, and love to service. And so, if they are not touched by the poor, it's because they do not know them.

I try to give to the poor people for love what the rich could get for money. No, I wouldn't touch a leper for a thousand pounds; yet I willingly cure him for the love of God.

Keep giving Jesus to your people, not by words, but by your example, by your being in love with Jesus, by radiating His holiness and spreading His fragrance of love everywhere you go. Just keep the joy of Jesus as your strength. Be happy and at peace. Accept whatever He gives – and give whatever He takes with a big smile. You belong to Him. Tell Him: "I am Yours, and if You cut me to pieces, every single piece will be only all Yours." Let Jesus be the victim and the priest in you.

Our works are only an expression of our love for Christ. Our hearts need to be full of love for Him, and since we have to express that love in action, naturally then the poorest of the poor are the means of expressing our love for God . . . A Hindu gentleman said that they and we are doing social work, and the difference between them and us is that they are doing it for something, and we are doing it for Somebody.

This experience which we have by serving them, we must pass on to people who have not had that beautiful experience. It is one of the great rewards of our work.

God's work has to be done in His own way; and He has His own ways and means of making our work known. See what has happened throughout the world and how the Sisters have been accepted in places where nobody ever knew anything about them. They have been accepted where many other people find it difficult to live or to be. So I think this is God Himself proving that it is His work.

A Gift for God
pp. 46, 47, 50, 51, 61, 62

ONE HEART

I always say – and I don't get tired of repeating it – that love starts at home. I will never forget that I was in a country once where there were many Co-Workers, but two of the coordinators for the Co-Workers were very distant from each other. And they were husband and wife. They came to me and I told them, "I can't understand how you are able to give Jesus to others if you can't give Him to each other. How can you find Jesus hidden under the distressing appearance of the poor if you cannot see Him in each other?"

The husband and wife started up an endless argument. Both of them let out all their frustrations and hurts, saying everything they had to say. Then I interrupted. "Now that's enough. You have said everything that you needed to say. Let's go to Jesus so that you can tell Him all these things."

We went to the chapel and the two knelt down before the altar. After a few moments, the husband turned to his wife and said, "You are my only love in this world, the only one I love and have." Other things of that sort followed. It was all very beautiful.

Now all the Co-Workers there have changed for the better. Why? Because those in charge of the group have come to understand that if we don't accept Jesus in one another, we will not be able to give Him to others.

The very same thing happens in our congregation. All our homes should be little "Nazareths" where Jesus can come to rest for a while in our company, for the work we do is only a means and not an end in itself. No matter how beautiful the work may be, it is still just a simple means. After all, what matters is to belong to Jesus. The work we do is our love for Christ transformed into deeds. It is the same for you and for each one of your Co-Workers . . .

Each one of them has to face the fact that as Co-Workers they belong to Christ. When I speak to non-Christians, I tell them that they belong to God, and they understand me. They understand that we all belong to the one from whose hand we have all come. It is for this reason that we must be capable of letting Him live through our lives.

One Heart Full of Love
pp. 54–5

ASK AND YOU SHALL RECEIVE

Let's focus more on the things we ought to do in serving our husband, our wife, our children, our brothers – rather than on other people's shortcomings.

I feel that we too often focus only on the negative aspect of life, on what is bad. If we were more willing to see the good and the beautiful things that surround us, we would be able to transform our families. From there, we would change our next-door neighbours and then others who live in our neighbourhood or city. We would be able to bring peace and love to our world which hungers so much for these things.

I have another conviction that I want to share with you. Love begins at home, and every Co-Worker should try to make sure that deep family love abides in his or her home. Only when love abides at home can we share it with our next-door neighbour. Then it will show forth and you will be able to say to them, "Yes, love is here." And then you will be able to share it with everyone around you.

We don't need guns or bombs to bring peace to the world. We must share the peace that is in our own homes. I believe – and each of you is certainly aware of it – that every day we seem to have less and less time for sharing. There is even less time in our busy day to share a smile with those in our own families. There is no one at home to hug the children. Everyone is so busy! And the elderly are in nursing homes. There is no one at home to play with the children, to spend time with them. That's why so many children end up on the streets.

I think that our Co-Workers should consider it their duty to seek out those children and bring them home. In the United States, we started up a group of young people – even though they are not officially Co-Workers – who have heard the call to seek out these children, just like Mary, who went searching for the boy Jesus to bring him home after he had got lost and stayed in the temple. We must go and find these children and bring them home; for if the children return, the parents will be affected, also.

A certain priest I knew was right when he used to say, "The family that prays together, stays together." Our prayer also has this purpose. We need to be able to pray. We need prayer just like we need air. Without prayer, we can do nothing. Someone asked me a few days ago what advice I had for politicians. I don't like to get involved in politics, but my answer just popped out, "They should spend time on their knees. I think that would help them to become better statesmen."

This is what we need to do when we go to share with others. For example, every time we need to make a decision concerning our families, we need to pray. Jesus said, "Ask and you will receive. Seek and you will find. Knock and the door will be opened." Nothing will be denied you.

One Heart Full of Love
pp. 56–8

GIFT OF GOD

What can you and I give to our children? A deep faith, for the child is the greatest gift of God to the human family, to all nations. So let each one of us make just one resolution as a woman, as a mother, as a wife – let us resolve that not one single child, born or unborn, will be unwanted, unloved or uncared for. Begin this in your own home. Begin with your people, with your husband, with your wife and with your children. Make them feel the wonderful love that you have been created for; that is why you are a woman – to love and naturally to be loved. If you love, love comes. I have received so much love from the thousands and thousands of people that have come to us, that have died so beautifully. They have just gone home to God. I have given, but I have received much more and this is for me the greatest gift from God.

From an address to the World Union of
Catholic Women's Organisations
Bangalore January 1979

BLESSED ARE THE PEACEMAKERS

I think it is beautiful to pray the prayer of St Francis of Assisi which always surprises me very much. It is very fitting for each one of us, and I always wonder that over seven hundred years ago when St Francis of Assisi composed this prayer, the world had the same difficulties that we have today. This prayer fits our situation very nicely. I think some of you already have got it – so we will pray together:

Lord, make me a channel of Thy peace
that where there is hatred, I may bring love;
that where there is wrong, I may bring the spirit of
    forgiveness;
that where there is discord, I may bring harmony;
that where there is error, I may bring truth;
that where there is doubt, I may bring faith;
that where there is despair, I may bring hope;
that where there are shadows, I may bring light;
that where there is sadness, I may bring joy.

Lord, grant that I may seek rather
to comfort than to be comforted,
to understand than to be understood,
to love than to be loved; for
it is by forgetting self that one finds;
it is by forgiving that one is forgiven;
it is by dying that one awakens to eternal life.
Amen.

Let us thank God for this gift of peace, that reminds us that we have been created to live that peace, and that Jesus became man to bring that good news to the poor. The good news was peace to all of good will, and this is something that we all want – peace of heart.

When the Virgin Mary discovered that He had come into her life, she went in haste to give that good news to her cousin, Elizabeth. The child in the womb of Elizabeth leaped with joy. That little unborn child recognized the Prince of Peace. He recognized that Christ had come to bring the good news, for you and for me.

Christ died on the cross to show that greater love. He died for you and for me and for that leper, and for that man dying of hunger, and for that naked person lying in the streets, not only of Calcutta, but of Africa and New York, London and Oslo.

He insisted that we love one another, as He loves each of us. We read that in the Gospel. As the Father loved Him and He loved us, so we must love one another until it hurts. It is not enough for us to say, "I love God, but I do not love my neighbour." How can you love God, whom you do not see, if you do not love your neighbour whom you see, whom you touch, with whom you live?

From Mother Teresa's Nobel lecture
December 1979 Oslo, Norway

IN GOD'S CARE

Today the greatest destroyer of peace is abortion. And we who are standing here – our parents wanted us. We would not be here if our parents had done that to us.

Our children, we want them, we love them. But what of the millions? Many people are very, very concerned with the children of India, with the children of Africa where quite a number die, maybe of malnutrition, of hunger and so on, but millions are dying deliberately by the will of the mother. And this is what is the greatest destroyer of peace today. Because if a mother can kill her own child, what is left but for me to kill you and you to kill me? There is nothing between.

I appeal in India, I appeal everywhere: Let us bring the child back, and this year being the child's year: what have we done for the child? At the beginning of the year I spoke everywhere and I said: Let us make this the year that we make every single child, born and unborn, wanted. And today is the end of the year. Have we really made the children wanted?

We are fighting abortion by adoption. We have saved thousands of lives. We have sent word to all the clinics, to the hospitals, police stations: please don't destroy the child; we will take the child. We will take care of you, we will take the child from you, and we will get a home for the child. And we have a tremendous demand from families who have no children, that is the blessing of God for us. And also, we are doing another thing which is very beautiful. We are teaching our beggars, our leprosy patients, our slum dwellers, our people of the street, natural family planning.

And in Calcutta alone in six years – it is all in Calcutta – we have had 61,273 babies less from the families who would have had them, because they practise this natural way of abstaining, of self-control, out of love for each other. We teach them the temperature method, which is very beautiful, very simple. And our poor people understand. And you know what they have told me? Our family is healthy, our family is united, and we can have a baby whenever we want. So clear – those people in the street, those beggars – and I think that if our people can do that, how much more you and all the others who can know the ways and means, without destroying the life that God has created in us.

The poor people are very great people. They can teach us so many beautiful things. The other day one of them came to thank us, and said: "You people who have evolved chastity, you are the best people to teach us family planning. Because it is nothing more than self-control out of love for each other." And I think they said a beautiful sentence. And these are people who maybe have nothing to eat, maybe they have not a home to live in, but they are great people.

From Mother Teresa's Nobel lecture
December 1979 Oslo, Norway

MOTHER

A doctor told me the other day about a girl of fifteen in school uniform with books in her hand who went for an abortion on her way to school. How did that mother not teach that child? How did that school not teach that child?

Why are our young children taking drugs? Why are they in the streets of London and Rome and Bombay . . . why are they there? Because there's nobody in the home to receive them. Nobody in the home to love them – and the child is hungry for love. There is no child that doesn't hunger for love – and I have seen very often in a grown-up woman that mark: when she was a child she didn't have love – a mother's love – and somehow the child is disabled, handicapped.

The other day I picked up a bundle from the street. I thought it was a bundle of clothes and it was a child. Somebody had left it there. Then I looked: legs, hands, everything was crippled. No wonder someone had left it like that. But who is the mother who did that? How can she face God? And this is her baby. But one thing I can tell you: the mother – a poor woman – left the child like that, but she did not kill the child, and this is something that we have to learn from our women, the love for the child.

Some days back I picked up a child and took her to our Children's Home, gave her a good bath, clean clothes, everything, and then after one day the child ran away; and again the child was found by somebody else, and again the child ran away. Then I said to the Sisters: "Listen, please follow that child, one of you, stay with that child all the time and see where it will go when it runs away." And then the third time the child ran away.

And then there under a tree there was the mother. She had put two stones under a small earthenware vessel. She was cooking something – something that she had picked up from the dustbins and the Sister asked the child: "Why did you run away from the home?" And the child said: "But this is home because this is where my mother is."

This was her home. Mother was there, that was home. That the food was taken from the dustbins was all right, because it was Mother that cooked it. It was Mother that hugged the child, Mother who wanted the child, it was the child who had the mother. Between the wife and the husband it is the same. He is the hands, he has to work. Are we there to receive him? With joy, with gratitude, with love.

From an address to the World Union of
Catholic Women's Organisations
Bangalore January 1979

111

THE PURITY OF MARY

The young people – especially today – need more and more the purity of Mary. It is very beautiful for a young girl to love a young man and for a young man to love a young girl. Love each other with a pure heart; the greatest gift you can give each other on the day of your marriage: ''a virgin heart, a virgin body, a virgin soul''. That is the most beautiful gift that they give each other. Some time ago two young people came to our house. They had just been married two days before and they brought me much money to feed the poor, because we feed over 9,000 people every day in Calcutta, and I asked them, ''Where did you get so much money?'' and they said, ''Before the wedding, we decided – we would not have wedding clothes, we would not have a wedding feast, but we would give you the money to feed the poor.'' I asked them, ''Why did you do that?'' They said, ''We loved each other so much that we wanted to give something special to each other.'' This love is sanctity and the more we grow in this love the more we become like Jesus.

Help the young people by your prayers to keep their bodies and their souls pure. What we see in the streets sometimes is not love – that's passion. Let us pray, let us ask Our Lady to give us her heart so beautiful, so pure, so immaculate. Her heart so full of humility; so that we may love Jesus as she loved Him, with a pure heart, with a heart full of love and compassion.

From an address to Co-Workers

WHAT LOVE CAN DO

The Sisters told me something very beautiful the other day in Rome; they go to jail amongst the young people and, there, a young Sister is preparing four or five of those criminal boys. There is a very wonderful chaplain in there who was so disheartened. Since the Sisters started visiting, he has started to have Adoration of the Blessed Sacrament for these people in jail. Well, it is something extraordinary, and, when I went to jail to see the people there, I told Father, "I can give you a beautiful monstrance if you begin Adoration in the jail." He said, "What on earth has happened to you, what do you mean, 'I will give you a monstrance?' " But, afterwards, he believed me and this has changed the whole attitude of some of those young boys of seventeen and sixteen that had never made their First Communion; it is so beautiful – I think some of them are making their First Communion today in the jail. Wonderful. See what love can do. This is really love in action.

From an address to Co-Workers in Dublin
June 1979

FRIENDS OF GOD

The young are the builders of tomorrow. Youth today is in search of selflessness, and when it finds it, is prepared to embrace it.

In Harlem a young woman of a wealthy family came to us in a taxicab and told me: "I have given everything to the poor and have come to follow Christ."

Sometimes Jesus receives unusual attention. One evening in London I had a telephone call from the police: "Mother Teresa, there is a woman in the streets very drunk, who is calling for you." We went to find her and on the way back she said to me: "Mother Teresa, Christ changed water into wine so that we would have some to drink." And she was very very drunk! . . .

If the individual thinks and believes that his or her way is the only way to God, if they do not know any other way, do not doubt and so do not feel the need to look elsewhere, then that is their way of salvation, the way that God comes into their life. But from the moment that a soul receives the grace to know God it must begin to seek. And if it does not seek, it moves away from the right road. But God gives to all souls that He creates a chance to meet Him and to accept Him or reject Him.

The Love of Christ
pp. 4–5

PAYING THE PRICE

Holiness consists in doing God's will joyfully. Faithfulness makes saints. The spiritual life is a union with Jesus: the divine and the human giving themselves to each other. The only thing Jesus asks of us is to give ourselves to Him, in total poverty, and total self-forgetfulness.

The first step towards holiness is the will to become holy. Through a firm and upright will we love God, we choose God, we hasten to God, we reach Him, we have Him.

Often, under the pretext of humility, of trust, of abandonment, we can forget to use the strength of our will.

Everything depends on these words: "I will" or "I will not." And into the expression "I will" I must put all my energy.

One cannot expect to become a saint without paying the price, and the price is much renunciation, much temptation, much struggle and persecution, and all sorts of sacrifices. One cannot love God except at the cost of oneself.

If you learn the art of self-restraint and thoughtfulness, you will become more and more like Christ. His heart is all recompense, and He always thought of others. Jesus went about only doing good. At Cana, our Blessed Mother thought only of the needs of others and made them known to Jesus. The thoughtfulness of Jesus, Mary, and Joseph was so great that they made Nazareth a privileged abode of the Most High. If we had this same solicitude for one another, our communities would truly become a privileged abode of the Most High.

The Love of Christ
pp. 20–21

GOING DOWN THE LADDER

It is our emptiness and lowliness that God needs and not our plenitude. These are a few of the ways we can practise humility:

Speak as little as possible of oneself.
Mind one's own business.
Avoid curiosity.
Do not want to manage other people's affairs.
Accept contradiction and correction cheerfully.

Pass over the mistakes of others.
Accept blame when innocent.
Yield to the will of others.
Accept insults and injuries.
Accept being slighted, forgotten, and disliked.
Be kind and gentle even under provocation.
Do not seek to be specially loved and admired.
Never stand on one's dignity.
Yield in discussion even though one is right.
Choose always the hardest.

The Love of Christ
p. 82

SUNSHINE IN COMMUNITY

Cheerfulness should be one of the main points of our religious life. A cheerful religious is like sunshine in a community. Cheerfulness is a sign of a generous person. It is often a cloak that hides a life of sacrifice. A person who has this gift of cheerfulness often reaches great heights of perfection. Let the sick and suffering find us real angels of comfort and consolation. Why has the work in the slums been blessed by God? Not on account of any personal qualities but on account of the joy the Sisters radiate. What we have – faith and the conviction that we are the beloved children of God – people in the world have not got, much less the people in the slums. The surest way to preach Christianity to the pagan is by our cheerfulness. What would our life be if the sisters were unhappy? Slavery and nothing else. We would do the work but we would attract nobody. This moodiness, heaviness, sadness, is a very easy way to tepidity, the mother of all evil.

If you are cheerful, have no fear of tepidity. Joy shines in the eyes, comes out in the speech and walk. You cannot keep it in for it bubbles out. When people see the habitual happiness in your eyes, it will make them realize they are the loved children of God. Every holy soul at times has great interior trials and darkness, but if we want others to realize that Jesus is there, we must be convinced of it ourselves. Just imagine a Sister going to the slums with a sad face and heavy step. What would her presence bring to these people? Only greater depression.

Joy is very infectious; therefore, be always full of joy when you go among the poor. That cheerfulness, according to St Bonaventure, has been given to man that he may rejoice in God in the hope of eternal good and at the sight of God's benefits; that he may rejoice in his neighbour's prosperity, take a delight in praising God and doing good works and feel disgust for all vain and useless things.

"It would be equally extraordinary," says St Ignatius, "to see a religious who seeks nothing but God sad, as to see one who seeks everything but God happy."

The Love of Christ
pp. 104–5

HUNGRY FOR LOVE?

To be able to love we need to have a clean heart. We get a clean heart if we pray. Prayer is that beautiful contact with God. We listen to God in our hearts and then we speak to God from our hearts. That listening, that speaking, is prayer.

And where does this love and this prayer begin? It begins at home. The family that prays together, stays together. And if you stay together you will love one another as God loves each one of you.

Spend at least a half-hour every day in prayer alone with God. This will purify your hearts and give you the light and the means to deal with all people with love and respect. For the fruit of prayer is always deep love, deep compassion, and it always brings us close to each other.

We know that Jesus Christ came into the world just to prove that love. And how He loved us! We know the cross. We look at the cross and we know THAT was His love for us. So let us love until it hurts. It is not how much we give but how much love we put into the giving, how much we are close to each other, that matters.

Make it possible for your families, for people, to look up and follow you, follow your example of love and joy and peace. Let us help each other in loving one another. Come to know your poor people. Help the Sisters. Help them to have a place where everyone can come, where all who feel unwanted, unloved, can come and feel wanted, feel loved. Then work with Him; do it all to Him, for Him and in Him.

Let us pray together that God's blessing be always with us, that we may come to know each other, love each other, serve each other, and, together, give our hands to serve the poor and our hearts to love them. God bless you.

Co-Workers' Newsletter
1982

I LOVE YOU

When the time comes and we cannot pray it is very simple: if Jesus is in my heart let Him pray, let me allow Him to pray in me, to talk to His Father in the silence of my heart. If I cannot speak, He will speak; if I cannot pray, He will pray. That's why we should often say, "Jesus in my heart, I believe in Your faithful love for me." And often we should be in that unity with Him, and when we have nothing to give – let us give Him that nothingness. When we cannot pray – let us give that inability to Him. There is one thing that we can do: we can let Him pray in us to the Father. Let us ask Him to pray in us, for no one knows the Father better than He, no one can pray better than Jesus. And if my heart is pure, if in my heart Jesus is alive, if my heart is a tabernacle of the living God: Jesus and I are one. He prays in me, He thinks in me, He works with me and through me, He uses my tongue to speak, He uses my brains to think, He uses my hand to touch Him in the broken body.

Jesus wanted to pray with a clean heart, with a simple heart, with a humble heart. "Unless you become little children you cannot learn to pray, you cannot enter heaven, you cannot see God." To become a little child you need to be one with the Father, to love the Father, to be at peace with the Father, our Father.

Co-Workers' Newsletter
1982

Is not our mission to bring God to the poor in the streets? Not a dead God but a living God, a God of love. The apostles said: ''We will devote ourselves to prayer and to the ministry of the Word.''

The more we receive in our silent prayer, the more we can give in our active life. Silence gives us a new way of looking at everything. We need this silence in order to touch souls. The essential thing is not what we say but what God says to us and what He says through us.

Jesus is always waiting for us in silence. *In this silence He listens to us; it is there that He speaks to our souls.* And there, we hear His voice. Interior silence is very difficult, but we must make the effort to pray. In this silence we find a new energy and a real unity. God's energy becomes ours, allowing us to perform things well. There is unity of our thoughts with His thoughts, unity of our prayers with His prayers, unity of our actions with His actions, of our life with His life.

Our words are useless unless they come from the bottom of the heart. Words that do not give the light of Christ only make the darkness worse.

Make every effort to walk in the presence of God, to see God in everyone you meet, and to live your morning meditation throughout the day. In the streets in particular, radiate the joy of belonging to God, of living with Him and being His. For this reason, in the streets, in the shelters, in your work, you should always be praying with all your heart and all your soul. Maintain the silence that Jesus maintained for thirty years at Nazareth, and that He still maintains in the tabernacle, interceding for us. Pray like the Virgin Mary, who kept all things in her heart through prayer and meditation, and still does, as mediatrix of all graces.

Christ's teaching is so simple that even a little child can learn it. The apostles said: "Teach us to pray." Jesus answered: "When you pray, say, Our Father . . ."

The Love of Christ
pp. 8–10

GOD'S GRACE, MY WILL

What is our spiritual life? A love union with Jesus . . . the divine and the human give themselves completely to one another.

". . . Thou shalt love the Lord thy God with thy whole heart, with thy whole soul and with thy whole mind." This is the commandment of the great God, and He cannot command the impossible. Love is a fruit in season at all times and within reach of every hand. Anyone may gather it and no limit is set. Everyone can reach this love through meditation, spirit of prayer and sacrifice, by an intense inner life.

. . . It is not possible to engage in the direct apostolate without being a soul of prayer. We must be aware of oneness with Christ, as He was aware of oneness with His Father. Our activity is truly apostolic only in so far as we permit Him to work in us and through us, with His power, with His desire, with His love. We must become holy, not because we want to feel holy, but because Christ must be able to live His life fully in us. We are to be all love, all faith, all purity, for the sake of the poor we serve. And once we have learned to seek God and His will, our contacts with the poor will become the means of great sanctity to ourselves and to others . . .

. . . Love to pray – feel often during the day the need for prayer and take the trouble to pray. Prayer enlarges the heart until it is capable of containing God's gift of Himself. Ask and seek, and your heart will grow big enough to receive Him and keep Him as your own . . .

. . . Our progress in holiness depends on God and ourselves – on God's grace and on our will to be holy. We must have a real living determination to reach holiness. "I will be a saint" means I will despoil myself of all that is not God; I will strip my heart of all created things; I will live in poverty and detachment; I will renounce my will, my inclinations, my whims and fancies, and make myself a willing slave to the will of God . . .

Often under the pretext of humility, of confidence, of abandonment, have we not forgotten the use of our strong will? We must have a real living resolution to reach holiness. St Teresa says that Satan is terribly afraid of resolute souls. Everything depends on these two words: *I will* or *I will not*. Into this "*I will*", I must put all my energy. "*I will*" said St John Berchmans, St Stanislaus, St Margaret Mary, and they did become saints. What is a saint but a resolute soul, a soul that uses power plus action? Was not this what St Paul meant when he said: "I can do all things in Him who strengthens me"?

Unpublished

GOD DOES NOT FORCE HIMSELF

There was a lady, an Indian, a very rich lady, who came to see me. "Mother Teresa," she said, "I love you very much and I want to do something for you."

I said, "Yes. That would be most welcome."

"I have a great love for beautiful saris," she told me. "I always buy very expensive saris." Her saris cost eight hundred rupees. (Ours cost eight rupees.)

Then she told me that she bought a new sari every month.

So I said, "Let your saris share in the work. The next time you go to the market to buy a sari, you buy a sari of seven hundred, then six hundred, then five hundred. The rest can go for saris for the poor. Then each, less, less, until you come down to a sari of one hundred rupees." I didn't allow her to go lower.

For her, that was a big sacrifice. But it brought so much joy to her, and to the whole family, for they all had a share in it.

Faith is a gift of God,
    but God does not force himself.

Christians, Muslims, Hindus, believers and
    nonbelievers
have the opportunity with us to do works of love,
have the opportunity with us to share the joy of
    loving and come to realize God's presence.
Hindus become better Hindus.
Catholics become better Catholics.
Muslims become better Muslims.

Living the Word
pp. 102–3

THE PRAYER OF JESUS

I remember one day I visited a lady who had a very bad cancer. She had little children. I didn't know which was the greater agony, the agony of the body or the agony of leaving the children.

She was really dying, so I said to her, "You know this is but the kiss of Jesus. See, Jesus loves you so much, you have come so close to Jesus on the cross, that He can kiss you."

She joined her hands and said, "Mother Teresa, please tell Jesus to stop kissing me."

Sometimes you have to say to Jesus, "Please stop kissing me." Say it to Him. And when you feel generous, and you do not have too many things to offer up, say, "Jesus, keep on kissing me."

It was the apostles who asked, "Jesus, teach us how to pray" – because they saw Him so often pray and they knew that He was talking to His Father. What those hours of prayer must have been – we know only from that continual love of Jesus for His Father, "My Father!" And He taught His disciples a very simple way of talking to God Himself.

Before Jesus came, God was great in His majesty, great in His creation. And then when Jesus came He became one of us, because His Father loved the world so much that He gave His Son. And Jesus loved His Father and He wanted us to learn to pray by loving one another as the Father has loved Him.

"I love you", He kept on saying. "As the Father loved you, love Him." And His love was the cross, His love was the bread of life.

Living the Word
pp. 108–9

TO SERVE YOU

Dearest Lord, may I see you today and every day in the person of your sick, and, whilst nursing them, minister unto you.

Though you hide yourself behind the unattractive disguise of the irritable, the exacting, the unreasonable, may I still recognize you, and say:
"Jesus, my patient, how sweet it is to serve you."

Lord, give me this seeing faith, then my work will never be monotonous. I will ever find joy in humouring the fancies and gratifying the wishes of all poor sufferers.

O beloved sick, how doubly dear you are to me, when you personify Christ; and what a privilege is mine to be allowed to tend you.

Sweetest Lord, make me appreciative of the dignity of my high vocation, and its many responsibilities. Never permit me to disgrace it by giving way to coldness, unkindness, or impatience.

And O God, while you are Jesus, my patient, deign also to be to me a patient Jesus, bearing with my faults, looking only to my intention, which is to love and serve you in the person of each of your sick.

Lord, increase my faith, bless my efforts and work, now and for evermore.

Somethings Beautiful for God
pp. 74–5

FIRE OF LOVE

What does the Society expect of its members? To be Co-Workers of Christ in the slums. Where will we fulfil that aim? Not in the houses of the rich, but in the slums. That is our kingdom. That is Christ's kingdom and ours, the field we have to work in. If a boy leaves his father's field and goes to work in another, he is no longer his father's co-worker. Those who share everything are partners giving love for love, suffering for suffering. Jesus, you have given everything, life, blood, all. Now it is our turn. We should put everything into the field also.

. . . Our prayers should be burning words coming forth from the furnace of a heart filled with love.

. . . In our work we may often be caught in idle conversation or gossip. Let us be well on our guard for we may be caught while visiting families; we may talk about the private affairs of this or that one and so forget the real aim of our visit. We come to bring the peace of Christ but what if, instead, we are a cause of trouble? We must never allow people to speak against their neighbours. If we find that a family is in a bad mood and is sure to start their tale of uncharitableness, let us say a fervent prayer for them and say first a few things that may help them to think a little about God; then let us leave the place at once. We can do no good until their restless nerves are at peace. We must follow the same conduct with those who want to talk with the aim of wasting our precious time. If they are not in search of God, do not argue or answer their questions; leave them. Pray for them that they may see the light, but do not waste your time.

Hear Jesus your Co-Worker speak to you: ''I want you to be my fire of love amongst the poor, the sick, the dying and the little children. The poor, I want you to bring them to me.'' Learn this sentence by heart and when you are wanting in generosity, repeat it. We can refuse Christ just as we refuse others.

''I will not give You my hands to work with, my eyes to see with, my feet to walk with, my mind to study with, my heart to love with. You knock at the door but I will not open . . .'' That is to give a broken Christ, a lame Christ, a crooked Christ deformed by you. If you give this to the people, it is all they will have. If you want them to love Him, they must know Him first. Therefore, give the whole Christ, first to the Sisters, then to the people in the slums, a Christ full of zeal, love, joy, and sunshine.

Am I a dark light? a false light? a bulb without the connection, having no current, therefore shedding no radiance? Put your heart into being a bright light.

The Love of Christ
pp. 110–12

LORD, INCREASE MY FAITH

Jesus, my suffering Lord, grant that today and every day I may see You in the person of Your sick ones, and that in caring for them I may serve You. Grant also that even in the guise of the fretful, the demanding, the unreasonable, I may still recognize You and say: My suffering Jesus, how sweet it is to serve You.

Lord, give me this vision of faith, and my work will never become monotonous. I will find joy in indulging the moods and gratifying the desires of all the poor who suffer.

O dear sick one, how much dearer still you are to me

because you represent Christ. What a privilege I have to be able to tend to you.

Deign also to be to me a patient Jesus, overlooking my faults, seeing only my intentions, which are to love You and to serve You in the person of each of Your children who suffers. Lord, increase my faith.

Bless my efforts and my work, now and always.

The Love of Christ
pp. 7–8

GOOD AND BAD

Self-knowledge puts us on our knees, and it is very necessary for love. For knowledge of God gives love, and knowledge of self gives humility. St Augustine says: ''Fill yourselves first and then only will you be able to give to others.'' Self-knowledge is very necessary for confession. That is why the saints could say they were wicked criminals. They saw God and then saw themselves – and they saw the difference. Hence they were not surprised when anyone accused them, even falsely . . . Each one of you has plenty of good as well as plenty of bad in her. Let none glory in her success but refer all to God.

We must never think any one of us is indispensable. God has ways and means. He may allow everything to go upside down in the hands of a very talented and capable Sister. God sees only her love. She may exhaust herself, even kill herself with work, but unless her work is interwoven with love it is useless. God does not need her work. God will not ask that Sister how many books she has read, how many miracles she has worked, but He will ask her if she has done her best, for the love of Him . . .

If you are discouraged it is a sign of pride, because it shows you trust in your own powers. Never bother about people's opinions. Be humble and you will never be disturbed. Remember St Aloysius, who said he would continue to play billiards even if he knew he was going to die. Do you play well? Sleep well? Eat well? These are duties. Nothing is small for God.

. . . We have grown so used to each other that some think they are free to say anything to anybody at any time. They expect the Sisters to bear with their unkindness. Why not try first to hold your tongue? You know what you can do, but you do not know how much the other can bear.

The Love of Christ
pp. 113–14

THE HEART OF THE HOME

When the angel announced to Mary the coming of Christ, she only posed a question: she could not understand how she could take back the gift of herself that she had made to God. The angel explained it, and she understood immediately. Her lips uttered a beautiful response that asserted all that she was as a woman: "I am the servant of the Lord. Let it be done to me as you say."

God chose a woman to show his love and compassion towards the world. It was she, the woman, who gave evidence of her kindness by immediately sharing what she had just received. To say it in another way, she hastened to share the Eucharist.

We know well what happened to John the Baptist in the womb. In the presence of Christ he leaped for joy.

This is our gift as women. We have been created to be the centre and the heart of the family.

As St Thérèse of the Child Jesus once said, "I want to place myself in the heart of the church in order to offer love." You and I have been created for that same end: for loving and for that love, as Mary loved everywhere and at all times.

We too have to go and look for our children, just as Mary did when Jesus was lost. We must live through the worry of not knowing where our children are. The home is not a home without the child. We also discover the genuine Mary, full of tenderness, in the wedding feast at Cana. She was moved by seeing the newlyweds exposed to the humiliation of not having wine. That is why she said to Jesus, "They have no more wine."

I think this is the wonderful tenderness of a woman's heart: to be aware of the suffering of others and to try to spare them that suffering, as Mary did. Do you and I have that same tenderness in our hearts? Do we have Mary's eyes for discovering the needs of others?

Perhaps in our own homes: Are we able to perceive the needs of our parents, of our husband, of our children? Do our children come home with us, as Jesus went home with Mary his mother? Do we offer our children a home?

We know what happened to Mary, the mother full of tenderness and love who was never ashamed of proclaiming Jesus her son. Eventually everyone abandoned him. Mary stayed beside him.

Mary was not ashamed by the fact that Jesus was scourged, that his face was spat upon, that he was treated as a leper, as one unwanted, despised, hated by all. Because he was Jesus, her son. And there surfaced in her heart the deep tenderness of a mother.

Do we know how to stay beside our own in their suffering, in their humiliation? When our husband loses his job, what do we represent to him? Do we feel tenderness towards him? Do we understand his anguish?

When our children are pulled away from us and receive bad advice, do we feel that deep tenderness that makes us go after them in order to draw them towards us, to welcome them home kindly, and love them with all our hearts?

From an address on Women and the Eucharist
Eucharistic Congress
Philadelphia, August 1976

LOVE WITHOUT LIMITS

Mary proclaimed Jesus her son. At Calvary we see her standing upright – the mother of God, standing next to the cross.

What a deep faith she must have had because of her love for her son! To see Him dishonoured, unloved, an object of hatred. Yet, she stayed upright.

As the mother possesses her son, she possessed Him, knowing that He who belonged to her was at the same time her absolute master. She was not afraid to accept Him as her belonging.

Do we know how to consider our own as our belonging when they suffer, when they are discarded? Do we acknowledge our own as our family when they suffer? Do we realize the hunger they have for Jesus in the hunger they feel for a love that understands them?

This is the source of Mary's greatness: her understanding

love. You and I who are women – do we possess that great and magnificent thing, that love full of understanding?

This is the love I observe with amazement in our people, in the poor women who day after day discover suffering and accept it because of their love for their children. I have seen many fathers and mothers deprive themselves of many things – very many! – and even beg, in order for their children to have what is needed. I have seen fathers affectionately carry their abnormal children in their arms because those children are their own. I have seen mothers full of a very tender love towards their children.

I remember a mother of twelve children, the last of them terribly mutilated. It is impossible for me to describe that creature. I volunteered to welcome the child into our house, where there are many others in a similar condition.

The woman began to cry. "For God's sake, Mother," she said, "Don't tell me that. This creature is the greatest gift of God to me and my family. All our love is focused on her. Our lives would be empty if you took her from us."

Hers really was a love full of understanding and tenderness. Do we have a love like that today? Do we realize that our child, our husband, our wife, our father, our mother, our sister or brother, has a need for that understanding, for the warmth of our hand?

From an address on Women and the Eucharist
Eucharistic Congress
Philadelphia, August 1976

THE VINE AND THE BRANCHES

Charity begins at home. That is why our first effort should be to make our homes into a new Nazareth, where love and peace reign. This can only be accomplished when the family stays together and prays together.

The suffering of today's world is very great. I feel that much restlessness and suffering start with the family. The family today is becoming less united, is not praying together, is not sharing happiness, is beginning to fall apart.

You, our Co-Workers, have a magnificent opportunity together in the mission of living a life of love, peace, and unity. Through that life you can proclaim to all the world that Christ is alive . . .

Missionaries of Charity and the Co-Workers should live their lives to the fullest. We are contemplatives in the midst of the world because we touch Christ twenty-four hours a day. Our Eucharistic union with Christ should bear that fruit, since Jesus has said, "I am the vine, you are the branches" (John 15:5). Grapes are on the branches, not on the stalk. How great then is your responsibility and mine, the responsibility of us all, since the fruit will depend on the union of the branches to the vine!

Hence our union with Christ must be something real, not mere fantasy. It must be alive, deeply felt, the fruit of conviction. And it must bear fruit first of all in the family. If we do not love our family from within, and if we do not love our neighbour, then our life is a failure.

Christ has chosen you so that you will be able to live out precisely this great vocation: your loving vocation as Co-Workers. Why you and not others? Why me and not others? I do not know; it is a mystery. But being together should help us to deepen our knowledge of God, and that knowledge will lead us to love Him, and love will lead us to serve Him.

When you or I attempt to discover Christ's face in others, Jesus cannot deceive us. It was He who said, "I was hungry, I was naked, I was homeless . . ." (Matthew 25:35–37). And yet, above all, our duty is to care for our own children, for our own families, then for others.

There is much, much suffering in the world. The material suffering is the pain of hunger, of exile, of all kinds of misfortune. However, I believe that the greatest suffering is to feel alone, unwanted, unloved. It is the suffering of not having anyone, of having forgotten what human contact is, what human love is, what it means to be wanted, to be loved, to belong to some human group.

This can occur even in rich families. And that is why I stress our duty to carry out our mission of love to our families above all.

From a meeting of Co-Workers
Germany August 1976

LOVE FOR ALL SEASONS

Love is a fruit in season and out of season, without limits – a fruit that is available to all.

Are we convinced of Christ's love for us and of our love for Him? Is this conviction a sunbeam that increases the sap of life and makes petals of holiness bud? Is this conviction the rock on which holiness is built, in the service of the poor, delivering to them what we would like to offer to Christ Himself?

If we follow this path, our faith will grow; and through

our growing conviction, the pursuit of holiness will become our daily task.

God loves those to whom He can give more, those who expect more from Him, those who are open, those who sense their need and rely on Him for everything. Our works are just an expression of the growth of God's love in us. Therefore, he who is more united to God is the one who loves his neighbour more.

May the love of Christ be a living bond between every two of us. From that others will realize that we are true Missionaries of Charity.

It may happen that a mere smile, a short visit, the lighting of a lamp, writing a letter for a blind man, carrying a bucket of charcoal, offering a pair of sandals, reading the newspaper for someone – something small, very small – may, in fact, be our love of God in action.

Even if this year we should collect less money, much less, the important thing is that we continue to spread Christ's love. If we give Christ to him who is hungry – not only for bread but also for our love, for our presence, for our contact – then this year could well be the year of the real live explosion of the love that God brings to our earth.

Without God we can spread only pain and suffering around us.

Heart of Joy
pp. 71–2

KEEP YOUR LAMP BURNING

Do not think that love, in order to be genuine, has to be extraordinary. What we need is to love without getting tired.

How does a lamp burn? Through the continuous input

of small drops of oil. If the drops of oil run out, the light of the lamp will cease, and the bridegroom will say, "I do not know you" (Matthew 25:12).

My daughters, what are these drops of oil in our lamps? They are the small things of daily life: faithfulness, punctuality, small words of kindness, a thought for others, our way of being silent, of looking, of speaking, and of acting. These are the true drops of love that keep your religious life burning like a lively flame.

Do not look for Jesus away from yourselves. He is not out there; He is in you. Keep your lamp burning, and you will recognize Him.

Christ has wanted to share our life, our loneliness, our anguish, our death. All of that during the hardest night ever . . .

How happy would many be if they were offered the opportunity to serve personally the king of the world! Well, that is what we are doing. We can touch, serve, and love Christ every day of our lives.

Your work on behalf of the poor will be better carried out if you know how God wants you to carry it out, but you will have no way of knowing that, other than by obedience. Submit to your superiors, just like ivy. Ivy cannot live if it does not hold fast to something; you will not grow or live in holiness unless you hold fast to obedience.

Be faithful in small things because it is in them that your strength lies. Nothing is small for our good God, for He is great and we are small. That is why He lowers himself and cares to do small things, in order to offer us an opportunity to show Him our love. Since He does them, they are great things, they are infinite. Nothing He does can be small.

Heart of Joy
pp. 82–3

SOMETHING BEAUTIFUL FOR GOD

This Jesus who is hungry for love and for bread, this Jesus who is deprived of food and of human dignity, this Jesus who lacks a home and understanding love – this Jesus is present today everywhere in the world, even here in the United States. He is looking at you and me and asking, "Do you love me? Are you willing to wipe out this suffering, which is the suffering of thousands and thousands of human beings all over the world – beings who lack not only bread but love and who want to be understood and acknowledged as our brothers and sisters, who are created by the same loving hand of God?"

In India, in Africa, and even in the United States, there can be people who are sunk in loneliness. There can be people like that in our own house, in our own family. Are we aware of that?

Especially today, when the world is so busy and people are always in a hurry, it seems we have no time to smile at each other, to devote a little time to others, to our neighbour. And thus loneliness grows every day. How much loneliness there is in the homes of shut-ins, those who can't go out.

In order to do what they do, our Sisters need to know what poverty is. They need to know it as a way of life in order to know and love the poor.

That is why the Sisters have their religious vows. They commit themselves fully to Jesus, in order to love Him with an undivided love in chastity, through the freedom of their poverty, in full submission through obedience, and in an absolutely voluntary and gratuitous service to the poorest of the poor – that is to say, to Christ in His most humble appearance.

Our lives have to continuously feed on the Eucharist. If

we were not able to see Christ under the appearance of bread, neither would it be possible for us to discover Him under the humble appearances of the bruised bodies of the poor.

God's work needs both you and me. Let us carry out this work together. Let us all together do something beautiful for God. What you can do we cannot do, and what we are doing you cannot accomplish. Together we will be able to accomplish and fulfil something beautiful for God through our full commitment and through our loving trust and joy in service to God through service to the poorest poor.

From an address in Washington,
October 1975

JUDGE NOT

None of us has the right to condemn anyone. Even though we see some people doing something bad, we don't know why they are doing it. Jesus invites us not to pass judgement. Maybe we are the ones who have helped make them what they are. We need to realize that they are our brothers and sisters. That leper, that drunkard, that sick person is our brother because he too has been created for a greater love. This is something that we should never forget. Jesus Christ identifies himself with them and says, "Whatever you did to the least of my brethren, you did it to me." That leper, that alcoholic, that beggar is my brother. Perhaps it is because we haven't given them our understanding and love that they find themselves on the streets without love and care.

I believe that we should realize that poverty doesn't only consist in being hungry for bread, but rather it is a tremendous hunger for human dignity. We need to love and to be somebody for someone else. This is where we make our mistake and shove people aside. Not only have we denied the poor a piece of bread, but by thinking that they have no worth and leaving them abandoned in the streets, we have denied them the human dignity that is rightfully theirs as children of God. They are my brothers and sisters as long as they are there. And why am I not in their place? This should be a very important question. We could have been in their place without having received the love and affection that has been given to us. I will never forget an alcoholic who told me his story. He was a man who gave in to drinking so he could forget that he wasn't loved. I think we should examine our own consciences before judging the poor, be they poor in spirit or poor in material goods.

One Heart Full of Love
pp. 130–1

VISION OF FAITH

Dear Jesus,
Help me to spread Your fragrance wherever I go.
Flood my soul with Your Spirit and life.
Penetrate and possess my whole being so utterly
that my life may only be a radiance of Yours.
Shine through me and be so in me that every soul I come
   in contact with
may feel Your presence in my soul.

Let them look up,
and see no longer me,

but only Jesus!
Stay with me and then I will begin to shine as You shine,
so as to be a light to others.

The light, O Jesus,
will be all from You; none of it will be mine.
It will be You, shining on others through me.
Let me thus praise You in the way which You love best,
by shining on those around me.
Let me preach You without preaching, not by words but
    by example,
by the catching force, the sympathetic influence of what I do,
the evident fullness of the love
my heart bears for you. Amen.

O Jesus, You who suffer,
grant that today and every day I may be able to see You
in the person of Your sick ones and that, by offering
them my care, I may serve You.
Grant that, even if You are hidden under the unattractive
    disguise
of anger, of crime, or of madness,
I may recognize You and say,
"Jesus, You who suffer, how sweet it is to serve You."
Give me, Lord, this vision of faith,
and my work will never be monotonous.
I will find joy in harbouring
the small whims and desires of all the poor who suffer.
Dear sick one, you are still more beloved to me
because you represent Christ.
What a privilege I am granted in being able to take care
of you!
O God, since You are Jesus who suffers,
deign to be for me also
a Jesus who is patient, indulgent with my faults,

who only looks at my intentions,
which are to love You and to serve You
in the person of each of these children of Yours who
suffer.
Lord, increase my faith.
Bless my efforts and my work,
now and for ever.

Heart of Joy
pp. 10, 141